How Senior Executives Make Poor Decisions When Selecting Senior-Level Direct

Reports

by

Roy C. Whitmore

Abstract

This qualitative study focuses on senior executives' perceptions of factors, including heuristics that influence their decision-making process when selecting senior-level executives as direct reports. Kahneman and Tversky found systematic decision-making biases, such as individual use of anchor points, supporting evidence, overconfidence, and perceptual effects (as cited in Flaming, 2007). Kahneman and Tversky's research on biases continued to define the issues they found with individuals' inherent preferences (Plous, 1993). For example, the effectiveness or comparable value of a decision can change based on the framing of a decision (Barkan & Busemeyer, 2003; Wang, 2004). Forlani (2002) argued that an individual's risk predispositions will differ based on the perceived outcome in a particular decision making domain. More recently researchers have confirmed that errors in subjects' decision making follow systematic and predictable patterns because of the use of heuristics (Rehak, Adams, & Belanger, 2010). These findings suggest that for senior executives' critical decisions to be effective, they must find ways to minimize their limitations, and heuristics.

Decision-making theory and research has focused largely on the actual decision and its outcome rather than the process itself, or *how* that decision is made (Boumans, 2008; Brehmer, Jungerman, Lourens, & Sevon, 1986; Lorge, Fox, Davitz, & Brenner,

1958). Further, much research dealing with human judgment has focused on the effectiveness of group decision-making or top management teams rather than individuals (Arendt, Priem, & Ndofor, 2005; Baker, 2010).

In this study, senior executives' responses to the interview protocol revealed that they use heuristics during their naturalistic and rational decision-making process for selecting senior-level direct reports. Additionally, this research identified the attributes that the senior executive participants in this study associate with the responses of senior-level executive candidates, during a one-hour interview, that often times assist them in accessing heuristics when making the final hiring decision.

Common themes that emerged from this research analysis included (a) the conceptualization of how senior executives use heuristics during their naturalistic and rational decision-making approach for selecting senior-level executives as their direct reports, (b) senior executives use heuristics to define and determine a senior-level executive's cultural fit, (c) senior executives use heuristics to determine personality fit and leadership style of potential senior-level direct reports, (d) senior executives apply heuristics and a rational decision-making approach to determine if a candidate's experience, previous contributions, and education are a fit for their organization, and (e) senior executives are overconfident of their decision-making process for selecting senior-level direct reports because of previous success.

Key Words: heuristics, senior executive, senior-level executive, culture, cognitive bias, values, Fortune 1000

Copyright by

Roy C. Whitmore

2013

ACKNOWLEDGEMENTS

My doctoral journey has been a real eye opener. I started this trip expecting the journey to take me directly to the PhD award in just a few short years, just as I did with my first advanced degree. However, I quickly realized that this journey is different. This journey is not just about learning but it is about creating something new, and it is about growing beyond your own imagination. I can say today that I have become that which I have searched for the last six years. I have become an enlightened person with a much deeper appreciation of those that I encounter and engage each day. I have become the real Roy Whitmore.

To my committee: Barbara Mink, Chair; Mary McCall and Keith Melville, Faculty readers; Terry Britton, Student Reader, and Barbara Adams, External Examiner – thank you for sharing your knowledge, experience, and critical feedback.

To those mentors and friends that offered great support and written and verbal suggestions that helped me make this document come to life the last 3 years, Keith Kraseman, Catherine Maraienau, Tony DiSandro, and Warren Roberts. Many thanks to the late John Willets, the mentor that always believed in my destiny to obtain this PhD.

A special thanks to Jackie Eder-Van Hook and my friend the late Charlie Seashore, your kindness and unconditional support can never be repaid. Thanks to the many faculty and friends from Fielding that made this day possible. Thank you Leonard Baca, Jeremy

Shapiro, Bob Silverman, Fred Steier, David Willis, and Dawn Sieh. This dissertation would have been much more difficult without the best editor ever Elyse Kutz, thank you.

Thanks to my wife Dot, my greatest supporter, love, and friend. It has indeed been a challenging 6-year journey and you have been by my side every step of the way. In many ways this is a shared accomplishments and one that you earned equally.

TABLE OF CONTENTS

Chapter 1:	INTRODUCTION	1
	Background of the Study	2
	Purpose of the Study	6
	Outline for the Dissertation	7
Chapter 2:	REVIEW OF THE LITERATURE	9
	Senior Executive Decision-Making in Selecting Direct Reports	10
	Hiring Practices	11
	Decision-Making Theory	14
	Heuristics and Cognitive Bias	22
	The Conceptualization and Role of Heuristics in Decision-Making	26
	Statement of the Problem	30
	Research Question	32
	Significance of the Study	34
	Definitions of Terms	35
	Assumptions	36
	Limitations	36
	Delimitations	37
	Summary	37
Chapter 3:	METHODS	40
	Introduction	40

	Research Design and Methodology	40
	Research Question	42
	Target Population and Selection Criteria	43
	Sampling Strategies and Recruitment	43
	Interview Protocol	44
	Ethical Considerations	45
	Procedures	47
	Data Analysis	48
	Chapter Summary	58
Chapter 4:	RESULTS	59
	Introduction	59
	Participants	59
	Bias and Heuristics Overview	63
	Findings	64
	Summary	87
Chapter 5:	CONCLUSIONS AND RECOMMENDATIONS	90
	Introduction	90
	Heuristics in Decision-Making	91
	Cultural and Personality Fit	92
	Leadership Style	95
	Bias	98
	Senior Executive Overconfidence Bias	99
	Personal Observations	100

Discussion	101
Implications for Practice	103
Implications for Theory	105
Recommendations for Further Research	106
Summary of Findings	109
Conclusion	111
REFERENCES	112

LIST OF TABLES AND FIGURES

Table 1	Ten Prevalent Heuristics, Their Definitions, and Participant Examples	52
Table 2	Participants' Use of Heuristics for Cultural Fit	77
Table 3	Participants' Use of Decision-Making Approaches and Applied Heuristics	82

LIST OF APPENDICES

Appendix A	Email Letter to Participants	130
Appendix B	Follow Up Letter to Participants	131
Appendix C	Thank You Email Letter To Participants With Copy Of Transcription	132
Appendix D	Interview Protocol	133
Appendix E	Transcriptionist Confidentiality Agreement	134
Appendix F	Fielding Graduate University Informed Consent	135
Appendix G	Categories and Heuristics Relationship	139
Appendix H	Coding Of Study Results	140
Appendix I	Atlas.ti Related Data and Family of Codes	140

CHAPTER ONE: INTRODUCTION

Hiring the right person for the right job is an expected maxim used by all senior executives in Fortune 1000 organizations today. In fact, most senior executives claim that the quest to find the senior-level executive for the right job that fits the culture and values of the organization is a primary ideology when selecting senior-level talent. Yet, identifying the right talent for a senior-level position by senior executives is a complex challenge that all senior executives face when hiring new senior-level direct reports for their organization. The senior executives' concern is that they feel the need to select a senior-level executive that possesses the right knowledge, skills, and both person and organizational fit. That usually means assessing whether the individual's technical skill set is compatible with the job requirements (Wolf, 2007). However, because the candidate's skills have usually been assessed prior to interaction with the senior executive, verifying the candidate's skills is of less importance during the senior executive's final decision-making process. Consequently, during the decision-making process for selecting a senior-level direct report, the senior executive is interested in understanding conceptually whether the candidate's values and personal attributes will be compatible with those of the organization and their peers (Wolf, 2007). This is a challenging decision for the senior executive. Accordingly, it is important to understand how senior executives use heuristics in their efforts to make the right decision in selecting senior-level direct reports. In addition it is important to understand what the qualitative content of their decision-making process will reveal. This study examines how senior executives use heuristics in their decision-making process to select senior-level direct reports.

Background of the Study

In addition to senior executive concerns regarding making the right decision when selecting a senior-level direct report, determining just how individuals make such decisions has been a research topic for over five decades of studies in the fields of cognitive science and social psychology. These studies have provided portraits of individual expert and novice decision makers in varied experimental and real-world settings (DeGroot, 1965; Simon, 1996; Zsambok & Klein, 1997). Studies of organizational factors that influence team and individual decision making in business have identified some key decision resources and constraints (Bazerman, 2001; Kerr & Tinsdale, 2004). A few studies have focused on the outcome of the decisions made by senior executives with mathematically based forecasting models and conceptual descriptions of organizational influences (Botvinick, Kool, McGuire, & Rosen, 2010). Findings from these studies illustrate the complexity of influences that appear to impact individual expert decision makers in complex real-world and laboratory settings. No one, however, has studied how senior executives use heuristics in their decision-making process for selecting senior-level direct reports. In light of changing workplace demographics and the current makeup of senior-level executives in Fortune 1000 organizations, conducting such a study to clarify how senior executives use heuristics in their decision-making process for selecting senior-level executives should prove valuable to organizations, senior executives, and those who aspire to senior-level leadership positions (Embrick, 2011).

Decision-making theory and research has focused largely on the actual decision and its outcome rather than the process itself, or *how* that decision is made (Boumans, 2008; Brehmer, Jungerman, Lourens, & Sevon, 1986; Lorge, Fox, Davitz, & Brenner,

1958). Further, much research dealing with human judgment has focused on the effectiveness of group decision-making or top management teams rather than individuals (Arendt, Priem, & Ndofor, 2005; Baker, 2010). Although groups such as executive search teams may initiate the interviewing process in hiring senior-level candidates, it is the senior executive who makes the final decision in selecting a senior-level direct report (Giberson et al., 2009).

Some studies have shown that culture and leadership traits have a profound influence on the senior-level executive selection process (Cable & Judge, 1997). Other research has shown that senior executives tend to promote junior colleagues who have similar backgrounds, beliefs, and worldviews (Giberson et al., 2009). Concerned about a good "fit," organizations often recruit individuals who share their cultural values and present traits that fit the culture of the organization. Senior leadership selection is a reflection of the organization's identity, which includes its culture, people, strategy, structure, and environment (Abebe, Angriawan, & Liu, 2010). Therefore, the decision-making process of senior executives for selecting senior-level executives as their direct reports is a critical part of supporting the identity and environment of the organization. The challenge these experts face is that of making the best decision during the senior-level executive selection process. Currently, senior executives make these decisions using their gut feelings, rule of thumb, intuition, experience, and disparate forms of heuristics (Rehak, et al., 2010; Simon, 1990; Shah & Oppenheimer, 2008).

Represented in the literature is the importance of the senior executive selection process to the success of executive teams and the organization. Selecting senior executives is a crucial organizational decision, and the corporation's senior executives are ultimately accountable for the selection of their executive teams in U.S. firms (Giberson et al., 2009; Walker & Larocco, 2004). Thus, the final responsibility for the makeup of corporate teams in Fortune 1000 organizations is that of the senior executives. The initial executive selection process is often shared with other executives, but the final hiring decision is the responsibility of the senior executive in the organization (Giberson et al., 2009). Hence, what is lacking from the literature is a general understanding of the elements of their decision-making process and how senior executives use heuristics in their effort to make the right decision for the organization qualitatively. Traditional decision-making theory and research focuses on the decisions made by rational people and the outcome of those decisions, not on *how* the decision is made (Brehmer, Jungerman, Lourens, & Sevon, 1986). Understanding how senior executives use heuristics in their decision-making process for selecting subordinates can add to the body of decision-making literature.

The decision-making performance of experts has been studied on the job and in laboratory settings (Carmeli, Tishler, & Edmondson, 2012; Zsambok & Klein, 1997). The results of these decision-making studies have generally supported these two distinct perspectives: (a) the rational (or classical) perspective, and (b) the naturalistic perspective (Rehak, Adams, & Belanger, 2010). The two decision-making models, rational-classical and naturalistic, follow from divergent assumptions about effective decision-making.

Simon (1996) proposed that two important premises shape the rational-classical approach to decision making. First, the best possible decision results from systematic exploration of available alternatives. Second, the purpose of decision making is to make the best possible or optimized decision. This requires extensive appraisal of each solution. The naturalistic model proceeds from different starting assumptions (Zsambok & Klein,

1997). Real-world experts are pressured by time, resource availability, and their own limited cognitive capabilities. Their goal is to make the best possible decision within all the constraints given. They tend to rely on solutions from past problems that best fit the current problem. Thus, the decision that emerges is an interactive product of the individual decision maker (relevant skill, prior experience, working cognitive capacity) with the specific problem and its context (Simon, 1990). Each decision model offers apparent strengths and limitations, with its effectiveness depending on available resources and constraints as well as on the skills and capabilities of the decision maker (Keller, Cokely, Katsikopoulos, & Wegwarth, 2010).

Rational decision theorists treat decision making as an extension of logic, where decision makers strive to achieve their highest valued outcomes using a comprehensive review of alternative solutions (Boumans, 2011). Research problems are often clear-cut, with direct goals and rules for achieving them, such as in chess or bridge (DeGroot, 1965; Lipshitz, Klein, Orasanu, & Salas, 2001). Simon (1969) proposed that individual cognitive resources offer a kind of bounded rationality due to the limits of memory and cognitive-processing capability. However, a variety of research studies have demonstrated apparent errors of judgment caused by systematic decision-making biases and heuristics (Rehak, Adams, & Belanger, 2010).

Simon (1990) declared that humans are uncomplicated and argued that the complexity of our environment has a profound influence on our behavior and decision-making ability. Insisting that humans are only partially rational, not having the capacity to fully grasp their complex environment and the uncertainty that surrounds the decision-making process, he developed the bounded rationality model. In his attempt to explain his decision-making theory of bounded rationality, Simon (1990) proposed that heuristics are methods for arriving at satisfactory solutions with modest amounts of computation, and humans seek to reduce the effort associated with the decision-making process.

While it has been demonstrated that the selection of senior-level executives is an important part of the senior executive's position, how do senior executives conceptualize the decision-making process for selecting senior-level executives as their direct reports, and how do heuristics inform that decision-making process?

Purpose of the Study

The purpose of this dissertation is to examine how senior executives use heuristics in their decision-making process for selecting senior-level executives as their direct reports. Understanding this process could assist in identifying qualitatively how they conceptualize the components of, and identify the heuristics that inform their decision-making process. Further, determining the importance that senior executives place on each component of their decision-making process could assist in improving their decision-making for selecting senior-level direct reports. Research by Cable and Judge (1997) purported that interviewers selected candidates based on person-organizational fit even after controlling for characteristics such as person-job fit. Giberson et al. (2009) proffered that the selection of senior-level executives is based on leadership traits that influence the culture of the organization. A number of studies have confirmed that leadership traits and cultural fit profoundly influence the executive selection process (Giberson et al., 2009; Schneider, 1987). However, these findings focus on the candidate and the expected outcome of the decision-making process. To date, no study has explored the components of the decision-making process of senior executives and their use of heuristics in their decision-making to select senior-level direct reports. Qing, Maruping, and Takeuchi (2006) suggest that the importance of selecting senior-level leaders that are a good organizational fit is a critical task that has profound implications for the future success of the organization. Therefore, understanding the use of heuristics in the decision-making process of senior executives for selecting senior-level direct reports encourages further investigation.

This study can offer multiple benefits. Senior executives will benefit from this study. Understanding qualitatively how senior executives perceive the elements of their decision-making process for selecting senior-level direct reports can offer alternative decision-making approaches during the selection process. This research will add to the body of literature that maps heuristics onto the decision-making construct. The study findings will benefit practitioners seeking senior-level executive positions by identifying leadership traits and abilities noted as desirable in direct reports by senior executives.

This study focuses on senior executives' perceptions of factors, including heuristics that influence their decisions when selecting senior-level executives as direct reports. A qualitative method was appropriate for this study as themes and patterns that develop from the data may identify strengths and shared beliefs and perceptions concerning how senior executives describe their decision-making process when selecting senior-level direct reports (Creswell, 2007, 2012; Fetterman, 2010).

Outline for the Dissertation

Chapter 1, Introduction provides a brief overview of the main focus of this study—How do senior executives use heuristics in their decision-making process for selecting senior-level executives as their direct reports? Background and purpose of the study were discussed. Chapter 2, Review of the Literature, provides a context for the study and reviews previous related research on decision-making theory and models as well as senior executive decision-making, organizational culture and related hiring practices, and heuristics and cognitive bias in decision-making. Chapter 3, Methodology, discusses the research method, design, assumptions, participant criteria and recruitment, interview protocol, ethical considerations, procedures, and data analysis, concluding with a chapter summary.

    Chapter 4, Findings, presents participant profiles and demographics and the study's findings. Five general themes emerged from the data and are discussed. The study's findings are discussed, within the framework of decision-making and heuristics literature, in chapter 5. Implications for practice, implications for theory, and recommendations for further research conclude the chapter.

CHAPTER TWO: REVIEW OF THE LITERATURE

Senior-level executive candidate selection is a critical task that can affect the success of an organization. Senior-level leaders are a reflection of the organization's identity, including its culture, people, strategy, structure, and environment (Carmeli, Gelbard, & Gefen, 2010; Carmeli, Schaubroeck, & Tishler, 2011; Carmeli, Tishler, & Edmondson, 2012; Hollenbeck, 2002). Additionally, a senior leader's sphere of influence can significantly impact the organization's employees, consumers, and shareholders. Senior executives are often in a position to succeed the CEO or President of the organization, and they impact its capabilities, human capital, and social structure (Qing, Maruping, & Takeuchi, 2006).

The initial executive selection process is often shared with others, such as executive search teams, but the senior executive is ultimately accountable for the final decision in selecting his or her executive team in U.S. corporations (Giberson et al., 2009; Walker & Larocco, 2004). Selecting the right fit in a senior-level executive is important for the long-term success of the organization (Da Silva, Hutcheson, & Wahl, 2010).

Research has shown that senior executives seldom rely on peer support when addressing critical decisions. They are concerned with sharing critical information with their team about issues within their businesses because of the potential influence on sales and profits. In fact, senior executives are reluctant to discuss certain corporate decisions with their executive team because of the possibility that such decisions could influence the staff's behavior negatively; discussing important decisions with peers from other companies is off limits because of competitive reasons (Frankl, 2010). Board members are there for support, though they are not available to address the daily challenges that senior executives face (Frankl, 2010, p. 5). They are alone at the top and they alone must make the decisions; as such, they end up using their intuition or rule of thumb to make critical decisions (Frankl, 2010; Gigerenzer & Hoffrage, 2008). Sometimes they are correct, but sometimes their decision-making process is flawed because of cognitive distortions leading to poor decisions (Rehak, Adams, & Belanger, 2010).

Senior Executive Decision Making in Selecting Direct Reports

Research has shown that senior executive activities such as environmental scanning and strategic decision making, including executive selection, affect organizational outcomes including structure and performance (Daft, Sormunen, & Parks, 1988; Priem & Harrison, 1994). In addition, a search of the literature showed several recent views on the importance of leadership traits that lead to job offers and promotions (Eagly & Carli, 2007). So too, Finn (2007) proposed that those personality traits that assist leaders in being successful were also traits that help leaders to attain promotions. Turk (2007) agreed, and exclaimed that the traits of a successful leader are traits that should be incorporated with vision. Turk asserted that some of those traits should include the ability to inspire and they should demonstrate excellent decision-making skills, as these traits could lead to senior-level promotions. Ericsson, Ander, and Cokely (2007) went further, arguing that to reach executive levels of performance leaders need to have traits that allow them to push beyond their abilities and comfort level, adding that the leadership traits that help leaders gain promotions include charisma, analyzing the wrong techniques used in organizations and making them right, and providing stewardship. This research, and a large body of previous studies, focuses on the job seeker. Conversely, there remains a void in the literature as to how senior executives decide who will be hired as their senior-level direct reports.

Hiring Practices

Research on hiring practices has shown that formalized hiring rules reduce the chances for gender or race inequalities during the hiring process (Castilla, 2008; Reskin & Bielby, 2005). However, when the organization's senior executive is making the final decision to select a senior-level direct report, formalized rules and procedures are not applicable and the decision-making process is guided by an unstructured matching of problems and solutions (March & Olsen, 1976). In such cases, the use of informal or biased criteria such as social similarity and social relationships is likely to have a more significant impact on employment outcomes (Gorman, 2005; Kalantari, 2010). For example, McIlwee and Robinson (1992) found that women were less successful in organizations where work was unstructured than in organizations where jobs were more routinized and rule-based.

Researchers have found that uncertainty leads decision makers to place greater weight on social characteristics and similarities when selecting candidates for employment, promotion, and other opportunities (Gorman, 2005; Pfeffer & Salancik, 1978). Individuals tend to be drawn to others like themselves, in part because similarity leads to attraction (Da Silva, Hutcheson, & Wahl, 2010; Schneider, 1987). Interaction and communication is easier with individuals like ourselves (Baron & Pfeffer, 1994; Bean et al., in press; Schneider, 1987). Research has shown that people develop a greater level of interpersonal trust and understanding with those who share similar ethnic, racial, or gender characteristics (Iberra, 1992; Marsden, 1987; Ruef, Aldrich, & Carter, 2003). The tendency to like and trust others who share social similarities is particularly strong in situations that are uncertain (Pfeffer & Salancik, 1978), for example, selecting executive-level individuals who will prove to be a good fit for an organization. Recent research has shown that cognitive biases in employment decisions are likely to increase in conditions where there is more managerial discretion (Dencker, 2008; Petersen & Saporta, 2004). Hiring managers tend to be socially influenced and hire, promote, and reward persons with similar social backgrounds, unless their cognitive biases are checked (Yechiam, Druyan, & Ert, 2008).

Organizational Culture and Hiring Practices

Researchers have noted the importance of leadership traits, particularly in individuals in upper management, which influence the culture of an organization (Giberson et al., 2009; Schein, 2004; Trice & Beyer, 1993). A number of studies have found that leadership traits and culture profoundly influence the executive selection process. Leaders and individuals are attracted to cultures that are a "person-organization fit" (Giberson et al., 2009; Schneider, 1987).

Research and theory in organizational culture and leadership emerged in the late 1980s to focus on the influence of values, meaning, interpretation, history and tradition, context, and symbolic elements in the leadership selection process (Bensimon, Neumann, & Birnbaum, 1989). More recent studies have examined how values and symbolic dimensions influence the leadership selection process, the way leadership is interpreted, and how leaders' beliefs shape their decision making (Giberson et al., 2009). However, few documented studies have described a leader's decision-making process and examined the content and process of leaders' decision-making when selecting senior-level direct reports.

Leadership scholars previously ignored cultural phenomena as they attempted to better understand leaders and the leader selection process. The evolution of the relationship between various cultural constructs and leadership selection supports the concept that organizational culture is a very important component of the leadership selection process, increasingly encompassing the study of values, gender, race, and cross-cultural issues (e.g., Banks, 1995; Bell, 1998; Cantor & Bernay, 1992; Giberson et al., 2009; Offermann & Phan, 2002; Valverde, 2003).

More recently, scholars have suggested that it is most important for organizations to match the makeup of their top management team to the strategies of the organization (Da Silva, Hutcheson, & Wahl, 2010) and the external environment. Scholars have suggested that both organizational leaders and the individuals who are pursuing leadership roles are seeking a fit based on shared values, mutual understanding, patterns of beliefs, and behavioral expectations that tie individuals together over time (Da Silva, Hutcheson, & Wahl, 2010; Schein, 2004; Trice & Beyer, 1993).

Certain organizational cultures are more attractive to certain types of individuals (Giberson et al., 2009; Da Silva, Hutcheson, & Wahl, 2010). For example, Schneider (1987) argued that individuals are drawn to organizations they perceive as having similar values to their own. He also proposed that senior executives of organizations recruit individuals who share their cultural values and who have traits that fit the organizational culture.

Schneider (1983a, 1983b, 1987) argued that organizations tend to become increasingly homogeneous over time because people are attracted to, selected by senior executives and retained within organizations that fit their personal preferences and characteristics. However, to date no one has researched how senior executives describe their decision-making process for selecting senior-level executives in an effort to understand how they use heuristics during this process. In fact, the construct of senior executive selection has generated increased attention during the past decade from academics, vocational organizations, and federal agencies alike (Braddock & McPartland, 1986; Embrick, 2011; Fernandez, 1999; Kirschenman & Neckerman, 1991; Royster, 2003; U.S. Department of Labor, 2010).

To make sense of this broad construct, this literature review provides a brief overview of decision-making theory and the role of heuristics during the decision-making process. It specifically expounds on the current research, scholarly arguments, and unanswered questions of the heuristics construct and the relationship it has in the senior-level executive selection decision.

Decision-Making Theory

Researchers have studied the decision-making performance of experts on the job and in laboratory settings (Chi, Glaser, & Farr, 1988; DeGroot, 1965; Zsambok & Klein, 1997). The results of these studies have generally supported two distinct perspectives developed from two schools of thought (a) the *rational (or classical) perspective*, and (b) the *naturalistic perspective* (Adams, et al., 2010). Studies of rational models developed from normative descriptions of how decisions should be made, and the resulting models were tested under controlled laboratory conditions (Cabantous, Gond, & Johnson-Cramer, 2008). In reaction to this approach, other researchers worked to describe how experts actually make decisions in workplace settings.

Research on decision-making styles by Brousseau, Driver, Hourihan, and Larsson (2006) reveals that seasoned executives (at senior levels) differ in their decision-making styles from lower level decision makers. Profiles of 120,000 managers and executives in a huge array of industries and companies ranging from Fortune 1000 to startups, found that approaches to decision-making for these executives differed in two predominant ways: in the way that people use information, and in the number of options they generate. The scope and implications of the most relevant models of decision-making will be discussed below.

Rational Decision-Making Model

Bernstein (2004) suggested that the roots of rational decision making date back to the Renaissance when Newton and other scientists believed that natural phenomena could be understood through the systematic study of nature. Logical-positivism, an analytic philosophy combining rationalism and empiricism, developed from this heritage and continues today (Kuhn, 1996). Rational decision theorists have argued that decision-making is an extension of logic, where decision makers apply logic while considering many alternative solutions (Boumans, 2011). Rational or classical decision-making models generally concentrate on an identifiable point, suggesting that decision makers utilize the most comprehensive and dependable evidence available (Flaming, 2007). They assert that following this model produces the best decision-making results (Lounsbury, 2008; Rehak, Adams, & Belanger, 2010). Rationalists' laboratory results were influenced by the prescriptive beliefs about formal, rational methods research designs where errors and successful behavior were defined by normative standards for successful performance and behavior (Boumans, 2011; Gigerenzer, 2000). These research problems were often well designed with clear rules and goals (DeGroot, 1965; Lipshitz, Klein, Orasanu, & Salas, 2001).

Hastie and Dawes (as cited in Flaming, 2007; Cabantous, Gond, & Johnson-Cramer, 2010) found that rationalist studies were intended to define how decision makers quantify problems with evidence, select options, collect data on options, and make a final decision following systematic approaches based on weighted averages. Researchers working with the rational model also studied the linkages and explanations connecting the final decision-to-decision alternatives in an input-output model to trace explicit influences (Lipshitz et al., 2001). Dawes, Faust, and Meehl (as cited in Flaming, 2007), argued that complex, rational models have delivered improved performance across multiple real-world entities.

Recent research continues with some of the early assumptions regarding problem structure or type following the early cognitive studies in which experts solved clearly structured, albeit complex problems where rules or scientifically proven outcomes guide the practitioners (Boumans, 2011; Croskerry, 2000; Kalantari, 2010). Decision making in such well-structured domains suggests that becoming an expert in this area is predominantly an outgrowth of subject matter learning and focused practice with feedback (Alexander, 2004). More recently, Rehak, Adams, and Belanger's (2010) review of the literature found that because humans are intrinsically subject to decision-making biases they are incapable of accounting for all factors that are relevant during a rational decision-making process because of their heuristics. In addition, they argued that individuals that follow the rational decision-making process are subject to human decision-making biases and errors that include availability bias, representativeness bias, confirmation bias, hindsight bias, overconfidence bias, framing bias, affect bias, and statistical bias (p. 327).

Bounded Rationality and Heuristics

Kuhn (1996) suggests that a second decision-making model was formed when unreliable data was derived from rational decision-making studies. Subjects were observed not following the concepts of rational decision making when cognitive psychologists began applying decision-making processes for transformation into scientific software programs (Chi et al., 1988). These observations shared similarities with previous studies when making real-world decisions. For example, researchers found that people purchased products for reasons other than price. When individuals attempted to apply an optimal decision making approach they often settled for a satisfactory solution rather than fully weighing all possible options when making decisions due to cognitive limitations (Hilbert, 2011; Plous, 1993; Simon, 1990). Simon (1969, 1990) proposed that individual cognitive resources offer a kind of *bounded rationality* due to the limits of memory and cognitive-processing capability.

Upper echelons theory takes a behavioral perspective in that it views the decisions of senior executives as made in a bounded rational way (Hambrick, 2007; Hambrick & Mason, 1984; Hilbert, 2011). Under such assumptions, the amount of information an executive has access to is overwhelming (Kalantari, 2010; Mitzberg, 1973), and an executive cannot optimize his or her decisions because of the information-processing requirements. Rather, the executive chooses a satisfactory course of action (March & Simon, 1958; Simon, 1947). Obtaining complete and or perfect information is simply too costly (in terms of time, resources, and foregone opportunities). Individuals must make choices that they can live with; heuristics permits them to do so (Kalantari, 2010). Bounded rationality challenges the assumptions of "rationality" of the decision maker and emphasizes his or her cognitive limitations, arguing that the outcome of such a process will be "satisficing," decisions which indicate that such decisions are not guaranteed to be optimal (Kalantari, 2010). In selecting alternatives, how an executive perceives information in the environment and how he or she makes choices is based upon individual cognitive biases and values (Hambrick & Mason, 1984; Hilbert, 2011).

A variety of research studies have demonstrated apparent errors of judgment caused by systematic decision-making biases (Palmarini, 1994; Plous, 1993; Rehak, Adams, & Belanger, 2010). Herbert Simon (1969), who won the Nobel Prize for his decision-making research, suggested that humans are psychologically disadvantaged as processors of large amounts of data by psychological limits in working memory. He observed individuals utilizing mental shortcuts or systematic strategies for rapidly reaching decisions with limited effort. Simon also found that individual subjects tended to sequence their decisions so they could focus on just one goal at a time, again suggesting a cognitive limit on their decision-making ability. When subjects attempted to apply the optimal approach to every decision, the pro-and-con analysis quickly resulted in decision paralysis (Gigerenzer, 2000; Simon, 1969). Another explanation of such bounded rational behavior was that as problems become more complex, measuring which preference or value motivated an individual's observable behavior became more difficult. Further, individuals were not always aware of their own preferences in making decisions (Croskerry, 2000; Rehak, Adams, & Belanger, 2010; Resnick, 2009).

Subsequently, Kahneman and Tversky (2000) received the Nobel Prize in

Economics for describing the everyday human decision-making process as systematically irrational. Kahneman and Tversky, further elaborating on Simon's work, conducted controlled experiments demonstrating that apparent cognitive-processing limitations, as well as the subject's attitudes and values, could account for a person's persistent biases. For example, the framing of a question could impact motivation to take a risk. Individuals were less likely to gamble when questions were framed in terms of losses, even if the net amount of money to be lost or gained was identical (Boumans, 2011; Tversky & Kahneman, 1974). The explanation of individuals' inherent preferences caused considerable debate. However, other research studies found that cognitive biases were the cause of systematic irrational decision making not an individual's inherent preferences (Lopes, 1997; Rehak, Adams, & Belanger, 2010).

Kahneman and Tversky found other systematic decision-making biases, such as individual use of anchor points, supporting evidence, overconfidence, and perceptual effects (as cited in Flaming, 2007). Kahneman and Tversky's research on biases continued to define the issues they found with individuals' inherent preferences (Plous, 1993). For example, the effectiveness or comparable value of a decision can change based on the framing of a decision (Barkan & Busemeyer, 2003; Wang, 2004). Forlani (2002) argued that an individual's risk predispositions will differ based on the perceived outcome in a particular decision making domain. More recently researchers have confirmed that errors in subjects' decision making follow systematic and predictable patterns because of the use of heuristics (Rehak, Adams, & Belanger, 2010). These findings suggest that for senior executives' critical decisions to be effective they must find ways to minimize their limitations and biases. A more in-depth discussion of judgmental bias appears in the

Cognitive Schemas and Heuristics subsection of this Literature Review.

Naturalistic and Other Decision-Making Models

Naturalistic decision making is based on observation, study, and description. Naturalistic decision makers often utilize rapid pattern matching, drawing from their experience with prior problems to reach a solution that is "good enough." When the task domain is highly structured and no new data is available to assist in closing the knowledge gap, decision makers take the first satisfactory alternative or they may rely on intuition (Kalantari, 2010; Simon, 1990). Klein's (as cited in Flaming, 2007) research found that the study of naturalistic decision making began as early as the 1930s, when Gestalt psychologists attempted to understand how patterns of comprehension "appeared in a sudden mental leap." Moreover, naturalistic decision-making research stresses that decision accuracy (e.g., hit rate) is not very important in decisions (Hoffman & Militello, 2008; Keller, Cokely, Katsikopoulos, & Wegwarth, 2010)

Shah and Oppenheimer (2008) suggest a different concept for comprehending the contribution of intuition in decision making that involves the use of heuristics or intuitive decision making, proposing the concept that heuristics reduce the effort associated with judgment and choice. Heuristics refers to the branch of knowledge that treats the art of discovery, learning, or problem-solving as experimental or trial-and-error methods (Merriam-Webster, 2012b). Shah and Oppenheimer (2008, p. 209) proposed that all heuristics rely on five methods of effort reduction that are in direct correlation to the weighted additive rule (a) examining fewer cues, (b) the difficulty of retrieving and storing cue values is reduced, (c) the weighting principles for cues are simplified, (d) less information is integrated, and (e) fewer alternatives are reviewed. Rehak, et al. (2010)

provided examples of decision heuristics (p. 324-327):

1. *Representative heuristics:* Occurs when individuals judge an event to be more similar to other cases.
2. *Availability heuristics*: Occurs when individuals judge an event to be more likely or frequent when an event is easy to recall.
3. *Confirmation heuristics*: is the human inclination to see what we expect and want to see from our environment.
4. *Overconfidence heuristics*: when individuals presume that their perceptions, abilities, and beliefs are more accurate than they really are.
5. *Anchoring heuristics:* Individuals often select a natural starting point by making a best guess for a first approximation and adjust from there.

Adams, et al. (2009) report that there is a large body of research that has explored naturalistic and intuitive forms of decision-making in real world environments. This research explains how decision makers can use heuristics to rapidly adapt their decisions to changing events in their complex environments. Researchers have found that the complexity of real-world issues appears to require a different type of expertise than is required in controlled laboratory settings. Furthermore, researchers argue that significant issues can arise because often times decision makers' are unaware of the heuristics that are influencing their decision making process during actual events. As a consequence they may use a shortcut or "rule of thumb" and accept a satisfactory solution (Shah & Oppenheimer, 2008). Rehak, et al. (2010) argued that the reliance on heuristics can help us to perform more efficiently and can also promote bias.

Cognitive heuristics are rules-of-thumb employed during decision making that can lead to biases that downgrade the quality of decisions (Keller, Cokely, Katsikopolous, & Wegwarth, 2010). Huey and Wickens (1993) identified how heuristics and biases impact decision making through the distortion of hypothesis formulation and situation awareness. They concluded that these distortions could occur throughout the cognitive task of information processing.

Heuristics and Cognitive Bias

Information Processing

Individuals process information in two general ways: *individual* and *categorical* (Fiske & Neuberg, 1990; Hastie, 1981; see Fiske & Taylor, 1991 for a full review). The individual process is controlled, and the individual attempts to attend to every detail with full attention. However, this process is very demanding and most managers lack the cognitive capacity to complete the process. Therefore, most decisions are hierarchical in nature, with input information processed by categories (Keller et al., 2010; Rehak, Adams, & Belanger, 2010; Simon, 1997).

Occasionally, however, categorization leads to systematic errors in judgment, which have been described as *cognitive biases* (Barnes, 1984; Rehak, Adams, & Belanger, 2010; Schwenk, 1984). Cognitive biases are predictable information-processing shortcuts that sometimes violate the rules of statistics and probability (Cyert & March, 1963; Hogarth, 1980; Rehak, Adams, & Belanger, 2010; Tversky & Kahneman, 1974). Certain biases systematically reduce an individual's risk perception and subsequently affect his or her higher decision (e.g., Barnes, 1984; Busenitz & Barney, 1997; Kalantari, 2010). Thus it is conceivable that executives may choose not to take a risk in hiring or promoting individuals who do not share their social, ethnic, or gender characteristics.

Hambrick (2007) proposes that senior executive' experiences, values, and personalities "affect their, (1) field of vision (the directions they look and listen), (2) selective perceptions (what they actually see and hear), and (3) interpretations (how they attach meaning to what they see and hear)" (p. 337). Given this dynamic, the same objective situation is seen differently, and results in different decisions from different individuals (Thomas & Simerly, 1994). Boone et al. (2004) suggest that although the importance of individual differences as determinants of behavior has long been recognized by psychologists, these differences are generally reflected in cognitive bias.

Past research framed bias in terms of heuristic modes of thinking in decisions and judgments (Rehak, Adams, & Belanger, 2010; Tversky & Kahneman, 2000). The starting point for theories of human judgment and decision making is that individuals have a limited capacity for mental work; hence, theorists developed several simple modes of reasoning and suggested that these heuristic modes of thinking can lead to bias and errors in decision making (p. 68). The cognitive heuristic principles used to simplify decision making sometimes lead to deviations from rational or normative models (Wickens, Lee, Liu, & Becker, 2004). These deviations or shortcuts can influence the quality of decisions, and lead to biases (Rehak, Adams, & Belanger, 2010).

Huey and Wickens' (1993) information-processing model identifies three major stages of information processing: *perception, processing*, and *responding*. Huey and Wickens suggested that information processing is an iterative process where each decision adds knowledge to the pre-existing long-term memory repository. Information in working memory is interpreted based on knowledge in long-term memory. Schemes are stored, making it easier to identify a familiar target. Over time, these schemes lead to the development of heuristic strategies meant to improve efficiency and validity of the information-processing function; however, the employment of these heuristics can also lead to poor decision making due to the presence of associated biases and predictable deviations from rationality (Rehak, Adams, & Belanger, 2010). This information-processing model is important to understand because of its broad applicability to numerous cognitive tasks including the decision-making process.

The literature suggests that because of humans' object identification process it is highly likely that biases will be present. Biederman's (1987) theory on human recognition of objects in two-dimensional images suggests that humans completing such a task are susceptible to cognitive biases. Biederman proposed their presence, as the final identification of the object is done by matching the human's perception of the object with what is held in his or her memory, acknowledging an exhaustive taxonomy of cognitive biases identified by decision theory researchers. This taxonomy of biases is divided into six broad categories: *memory, statistical, confidence, presentation, situation,* and *adjustment bias*. Multiple biases may be present at one time and work in conjunction with one another, and an attempt to eliminate one bias may create another (Biederman, 1987).

Cognitive Schemas and Heuristics

The growing body of research on judgment bias in leadership perception and leader selection suggests schemas are one explanation for judgment bias. Hilbert (2011) theorizes that the mind is the result of "biological evolution" and it does not seek perfection but a degree of competitiveness in its environment (p. 212). Because our minds are biologically limited and our information-processing system is imperfect, we depend on cognitive schemas and heuristics during our decision-making process (Hilbert, 2011).

Studies have shown that well-established race-related stereotypes exist in children's schema before children have the cognitive capacity or awareness to evaluate their validity (Allport, 1954). These schemas, along with prior knowledge, stereotypes, and the law of probability, confound memory inaccuracy that occurs during recall when individuals use top-down approach to retrieving fading data (Hicks, Marsh, & Ritschel, 2001). This is especially true for stereotypes. Reliance on stereotypes increases as memory fades during recall tasks (Spaniol & Bayen, 2001). One study showed that people make more stereotype-consistent errors, in contrast to stereotype-inconsistent errors, as time to recall elapsed (Kleider, Pezdek, Goldinger, & Kirk, 2008).

Cognitive schemas are structures considered to be useful for efficiently encoding, interpreting, and storing new information as well as retrieving old information (Lord & Maher, 1991). In general, the schema chosen to encode and interpret new information is based on a matching process between the salient features of the incoming information and the components or elements of a schema, which can lead to biased decisions (Fiske & Neuberg, 1990).

More recently researchers found that people regulate their behavior to coincide with their self-concept. The self-concept is the collection of beliefs that people hold about themselves (Baumeister, 1998). The self-concept refers to how people view themselves. For example, people think of themselves as liberal or conservative, reflecting the beliefs they hold regarding abortion and gun control among other issues. Although people can readily report how they view themselves, they tend not to spend much time thinking about or attending to themselves (Csikszentmihalyi & Figurski, 1982). In other words, people are typically not in a state of self-awareness.

Visual information (e.g., gender, race, physical appearance) has been found to be very significant (Brewer, 1988). Stangor, Lynch, Duan, and Glass (1992) found that visual gender information is one of the most salient kinds of information for schema activation. Visual information is usually processed quickly and automatically, resulting in immediate activation of relevant schemas. Concurrently, the activation of other competing schemas is repressed (Bechtel & Abrahamsen, 1991). Thus, visual information, such as gender or race, can drive the encoding of subsequent information and impact judgments and the decision-making process. Furthermore, there is a growing body of research suggesting that a target's race may influence early stages of attention (Correll, Urland, & Ito, 2006; Eberhardt, Goff, Purdie, & Davis, 2004). Bean et al. (in press) offer empirical evidence that individuals high in external motivation exhibit an early bias toward those that are different. In their study of 36 White undergraduates (18-24 years old) using eyetracking methodology, they found race-based attentional biases using an experimental paradigm where participants were unaware that a target's race was an important component of the task they were asked to complete (Bean et al., in press).

The Conceptualization and Role of Heuristics in Decision Making

Heuristics Defined

The Ancient Greeks first identified heuristics in decision making. Aristotle believed that humans could reason, and he examined the different forms this reasoning can take (Aristotle, 2007). Further, he conceded that not all reasoning was logical, admitting, for example, that an individual's experience was of great value when making decisions. It is believed that Aristotle was probably the first philosopher to use heuristics as semi-formalized logic (Frankl, 2010).

Newell and Simon (1972) are responsible for the term *heuristics* gaining broad attention in psychology when they used the term to describe an effortless process that replaced complex algorithms. Simon (1990), the father of heuristics research in judgment and decision making, argued that because people lack the capacity to compute large amounts of information, they find ways to arrive at satisfactory solutions. Originally the many challenges to human decision making were referred to as biases because the outcomes were moved away from the theoretical normative (Resnick, 2009). However, these biases have more recently been referred to as heuristics because they serve as shortcuts that deliver satisfactory solutions faster (Rehak, et al., 2010; Resnick, 2009).

Heuristics are not necessarily readily generalized and not necessarily always correct; they are practical principles with broad application, not necessarily always accurate. Heuristics can be clear, concise, and understandable processes, whereas others sound unfinished, vague, and even confusing because they acquire unspecified additional knowledge. Heuristics can provide adequate decision-making guidelines for senior executives when problem solving or when they are selecting senior-level executives as their direct reports, especially when critical information is missing or time is of the essence (Gigerenzer & Hoffrage, 2008). Resnick (2009) argued that even the use of the term *heuristics* could be inaccurate because heuristics imply that they are consciously applied and this is not always the case.

Heuristics-based problem-solving methods are present extensively in business, education, and in all areas of existence. These various methods are often difficult to define. Heuristics have often vague, even contradictory definitions in the present literature. The meaning of heuristics is different depending on the circumstance and environment to which one applies it. Frankl (2010) suggested that the use of heuristics is a speculative problem-solving process, useful in psychology, mathematics, astrophysics, and philosophy of science. Heuristics are interpreted in many ways some include trial-and- error handling; decision-making shortcuts, satisfactory solutions, unstructured proof, learning from experience, in comparison to previously recognized patterns, intelligent guesswork, speculative formulation, investigative discovery, rules of thumb, algorithmic search, and even common sense (Frankl, 2010; Rehak, Adams, & Belanger, 2010; Shah & Oppenheimer, 2008).

Hinkle and Kuehn (1966) found that early application of heuristics in business primarily took the form of statistical or quantitative analysis. When financial problems are present, senior executives have an abundance of financial and risk management tools available to assist them in their decision making process for selecting senior-level direct reports (Frankl, 2010). However, one cannot always quantify business risk (Coleman, 2006). How should executives respond when their perception of the problem is not quantifiable? They apply heuristics to their decision-making process in an effort to make the best qualitative decision (Hilbert, 2011; Kahneman, Slovic, & Tversky, 1982; Shah & Oppenheimer, 2008).

Most of the heuristics and biases have been identified in laboratory experiments using relatively structured tasks. As a result, strategic management researchers have attempted to identify examples of the operations of the heuristics and biases in actual strategic decisions. The focus on simplification processes involving both laboratory and field support increased the chance of identifying cognitive processes, which really do affect organizational decisions rather than artificially produced results from laboratories alone (Schwenk, 1995). Researchers have identified the heuristics and biases that are most prevalent during strategic and expert decision-making processes as availability heuristics, selective perception, conservatism, illusion heuristics, recognition heuristics, representativeness heuristics, and confirmation bias (Rehak, Adams, & Belanger, 2010; Schwenk, 1988; Shah & Oppenheimer, 2008). In-depth discussion of these individual heuristics is beyond the scope of this study, however some will be highlighted during the research phase.

The Role of Heuristics in Decision Making

Because informational constraints and daily challenges faced by executives originate from dilemmas that need immediate response, leaving little time for detailed analysis, there is a need for the use of heuristics-based decision making (Hilbert, 2011). Though heuristics can be a catalyst for cognitive biases and systematic errors, they can also be an effective decision-making strategy as a *computational algorithm* (Keller, Cokely, Katsikopoulos, & Wegwarth, 2010).

Simon (1990) suggests using simple rules for deciding how to use found information, like rules of syllogism in formal logic. Simon stressed that "because of the limits of their [computers and human brain included] computing speeds and power, intelligent systems must use approximate methods to handle most tasks. Their rationality is bounded" (p.6). Simon (1990) further advocates the use of heuristics for information search and for needing to stop the search.

On the other hand, research by Keller, Cokely, Katsikopoulos, and Wegwarth (2010) on naturalistic decision making (NDM) outside the laboratory confirmed that decision accuracy is not all that important in a decision. Gigerenzer and Hoffrage (2008), in their research at the Max Plank Institute for Human Development, found that applying heuristics for problem solving could lead to remarkably accurate solutions. However, no research has confirmed how heuristics can influence the decision-making process of senior executives when selecting senior-level direct reports.

Statement of the Problem

Ambiguity and uncertainty continues to exist today regarding how senior executives use heuristics in their decision-making process for selecting senior-level executives as their direct reports. Finkelstein (1992) suggested that power and accountability are not equally distributed among top management team members; often the senior executive retains the largest share of both and is ultimately responsible for selecting his or her direct reports (Hambrick & Mason, 1984). Though the initial decision during the senior-level executive selection process is shared with others, ultimately one senior executive will make the final decision to select his or her direct report (Giberson et al., 2009). Understanding senior executives' decision-making process for selecting senior-level executives, and how they use heuristics, can add to the body of research in decision making. Further, this knowledge can assist in clarifying the effects of heuristics during the decision-making process of senior executives when they are selecting their senior-level direct reports.

Research on the decision-making performance of experts has supported two distinct perspectives: (a) the rational (or classical) perspective, and (b) the naturalistic perspective. The rational generally focuses on the point of choice decision suggesting that decision makers utilize the most reliable evidence often times supported by quantitative heuristics (Hinkle & Kuehn, 1966; Rehak, Adams, & Belanger, 2010). Conversely, naturalistic decision makers often rely on heuristics using available information and experience with prior problems to reach a solution that is "good enough." Moreover, naturalistic decision-making research stresses that accuracy is not very important in decisions, and because executives often deal with incomplete information, qualitative heuristics can be helpful (Gigerenzer & Hoffrage, 2008; Keller, Cokely, Katsikopoulos, & Wegwarth, 2010).

However, even with the many conceptualizations and organizations of the decision-making construct by researchers, there remains a void in the literature in how senior executives use heuristics in their decision-making process qualitatively for selecting senior-level direct reports. As a result, the first research question will ask senior executives of Fortune 1000 organizations to define their decision-making process for selecting a senior-level direct report that was successful.

Secondly, the importance that the senior executives place on the elements of their decision-making process for selecting senior-level executives during the interview process warrants investigation. Such content could reveal the use of heuristics and identify which are most important during the selection process, for example, selecting the right fit in a senior-level executive (Da Silva, Hutcheson, & Wahl, 2010). Rehak, Adams, and Belanger (2010) posit that stored schemes lead to the development of heuristics strategies meant to improve efficiency and validity of the information-processing function during the decision-making process, but they also lead to predictable deviations from rationality. However, while research has explored the effects of heuristics during the decision-making process of experts (Zsambok & Klein, 1997), just how heuristics are used or what heuristics are involved in the decision-making process of senior executives when selecting their senior-level direct reports has not been recognized. They specifically explored the outcomes of using heuristics during the decision-making process. Their findings indicated that heuristics could influence the decision-making process both negatively and positively (Hilbert, 2011; Kalantari, 2010). In addition to the many conceptualizations of the decision-making processes of senior executives for selecting senior-level direct reports, multiple heuristics also exist. Some of the common definitions of heuristics include trial-and-error problem-solving process, computational algorithm, applied shortcuts, and "satisficing" rather than optimal (Hilbert, 2011; Kalantari, 2010; Keller, Cokely, Katsikopoulos, & Wegwarth, 2010; Simon, 1997). Other scholars have defined heuristics as information-processing shortcuts (Shah & Oppenheimer, 2008), rules of thumb (Tversky & Kahneman, 1974), and methods that use principles of effort-reduction and simplification (Shah & Oppenheimer, 2008).

In addition, past decision-making research has suggested that the senior executive decision-making process when interviewing candidates is influenced by characteristics of the candidate such as work experience, education, job knowledge, professionalism, values, and overall skills (Cable & Judge, 1997). A 2000 study by Kahneman and Tversky demonstrated that a subject's attitudes and values could influence the decision-making process and account for biases. Gigerenzer's (2000) research on decision-making explained how heuristics might affect the decision-making process and the outcome. However, current and past research has not qualitatively studied how senior executives use heuristics in their decision-making process for selecting senior-level direct reports.

Research Question

How do senior executives use heuristics in their decision-making process to select senior-level executives as direct reports?

Understanding how senior executives use heuristics in their decision-making process for selecting their senior-level direct reports will extend the body of decision-making literature. This research will also add to the literature that maps heuristics onto decision-making components to better understand their importance and effects on the decision-making process of senior executives when selecting senior-level direct reports.

For practitioners, this research will establish clarity regarding the executive selection process and assist in understanding the decision-making process of senior executives for selecting senior-level executives as their direct reports. Further, it will offer meaningful insight into how senior executives use heuristics during the decision-making process for selecting senior-level direct reports. This research will also offer future senior-level executives suggestions for preparing for such a role.

The research questions that guided this qualitative study are descriptive. Descriptive research questions are designed to enable understanding of how variables relate and interact with an experience (Neuman, 2006). Descriptive questions are appropriate for this study because the purpose is to understand how senior executives use heuristics in their decision-making process when selecting senior-level executives as their direct reports. Thus, the first question instructs the study participants as follows: *Think about a process you have used in making hiring and promotional decisions the last few years. I would like you to focus on an event that you experienced as going well, and tell me a bit about what you were thinking, how you were assessing and evaluating the candidate, and what elements of the process caused you to believe that you should hire this individual. It would help if you simply tell a story about the experience and I will occasionally ask you specific questions.*

With qualitative analysis, researchers use questions to condense information from the purpose statement into statements for answers sought (Fetterman, 2010). Qualitative researchers endeavor to identify multiple facets within their area of interest because they believe situations are complex (Creswell, 2012). The use of this research question will disclose information that will add to the current literature and provide additional knowledge to corporate leaders and researchers in the area of decision making by describing what heuristics are present and how they are used during senior executives' interviewing and selection process of senior-level executives as direct reports. For practitioners, it will provide insight into the characteristics that senior executives seek in their senior-level direct reports and establish a more equitable executive selection process for all senior-level executives as potential direct reports of senior executives in Fortune 1000 organizations (Fernandez, as cited in Embrick, 2011).

Significance of the Study

This study addresses a gap in the literature related to understanding how senior executives use heuristics in their decision-making process for selecting senior-level direct reports. To date, no investigation addresses this phenomenon qualitatively from the senior executive perspective. Further, it extends the literature related to the role of heuristics during the decision-making process. Overall, this research will add validity to the executive selection process construct, as well as the role and importance of the heuristic-based decision-making construct in organizational contexts when senior executives are considering senior-level candidates to be their direct reports.

Definitions of Terms

The creation of a research design requires knowledge of concepts and groupings to be studied (Fetterman, 2010). The key terms associated with this research are defined as follows:

Cognitive biases — A form of inaccurate judgment. "Human decision-making biases represent systematic rather than random errors, making biases somewhat predictable" (Gilovich, Griffin & Kahneman, 2002, as cited in Rehak, Adams, & Belanger, 2010, p. 324). Consequently, the key to biases, then, requires understanding why people are prone to select or encourage one outcome or answer over another in similar situations (Rehak, Adams, & Belanger, 2010).

Culture —The ideas, beliefs, and knowledge that characterize a particular group of people (Fetterman, 2010).

Fortune 500—The top 500 companies in the United States based on revenue. Many of these companies are America's most admired; for example, Apple, Microsoft, Walt Disney, General Electric, and Target stores.

Fortune 1000 —The top 1,000 companies in the United States based on revenue.

Heuristics — Heuristics are "methods for arriving at satisfactory solutions with modest amounts of computation," suggesting that people seek to reduce the effort associated with decision processes (Simon, 1990, p. 11)

Senior-Level Executive—As used in this study, an individual who has reached the title of vice president or above in a corporation, or an executive who is a direct report to the CEO or President and not more than three levels removed (Bacchus, 2004, p.13).

Values — are defined by Enz (1988) as being "the belief held by an individual or group regarding means and ends organizations 'ought to' or 'should' identify in the running enterprise. Values result in a preference for one behavior over another" (p. 287).

Assumptions

This qualitative research study has four basic assumptions: The first assumption is that the study participants provided sufficient data to produce extensive information related to the decision-making process of senior executives in hiring senior-level direct reports. The second assumption is that participants reflected on their executive experience concerning factors associated with selecting senior executives (Creswell, 2007). In maintaining the integrity of a qualitative research design, the third assumption is that any participant prejudgments of what constitutes the decision-making process when selecting subordinates were set aside to avoid bias (Creswell, 2012). The final assumption is that the purposive sample of 13 senior executives from Fortune 1000 corporations provided sufficient data related to how those individuals seeking senior-level executive positions might better prepare, thereby increasing their chances of obtaining a future senior executive position.

Limitations

There are several limitations to this research study. First, the study results are based on the perceptions of senior executive participants. Results are limited by the honesty of the participants' responses to interview questions based on their individual experience as senior executive of a Fortune 1000 corporation.

Another limitation in this study is that the researcher is an African American and former senior executive of two Fortune 1000 corporations; his presence could have influenced the recording process and perception of information obtained during the interview. To address this limitation, a transcriptionist with no connection to the research project was commissioned to transcribe the audiotaped interviews (see Appendix C).

An additional limitation of this study, the small sample size, limits the ability to generalize the research findings. Future studies that surmount the decision-making process of senior executives selecting direct reports for senior-level executive positions in Fortune 1000 organizations will be aided by the baseline information collected through this study.

Delimitations

Participants were limited to Fortune 1000 senior executives who are currently in that position or had held that position less than 5 years prior to the interview schedule of the study.

Summary

This study addresses the research question: How do senior executives use heuristics in their decision-making process for selecting senior-level executives as direct reports?

Senior executives must consider not only the candidate's technical skill set, but also whether he or she will be a "good fit" for the position as well as the culture of the organization. A team or search committee who determine that the candidate has the skills and experience to fit the job initially screens most senior-level executives. Thus, it ultimately becomes the responsibility of the senior executive to determine whether the candidate's values and behavior will be compatible with those of the organization, or whether he or she is a good fit.

Various studies have explored the importance of leadership and personality as sought-after traits in hiring senior-level executives (Eagly & Carli, 2007). Recent studies have shown the importance of matching the makeup of top management teams to the strategies of the organization (Da Silva, Hutcheson, & Wahl, 2010) and the external environment. Organizations are increasingly focusing on shared values, mutual understanding, patterns of beliefs, and behavioral expectations that tie individuals together over time (Da Silva, Hutcheson, & Wahl, 2010; Schein, 2004; Trice & Beyer, 1993).

Organizational culture is also an important component of the senior executive selection process, increasingly encompassing the study of values, gender, race, and cross-cultural issues (e.g., Banks, 1995; Bell, 1998; Cantor & Bernay, 1992; Giberson et al., 2009; Offermann & Phan, 2002; Valverde, 2003). Research has shown that people develop a greater level of interpersonal trust and understanding with those who share similar ethnic, racial, or gender characteristics (Iberra, 1992; Marsden, 1987; Ruef, Aldrich, & Carter, 2003), especially in situations that are uncertain (Pfeffer & Salancik, 1978), such as determining who will prove to be a good fit for an organization. Unfortunately, this may lead to cognitive bias.

Decision-making theory, including the rational (or classical) perspective and the naturalistic perspective, were discussed as related to the study's focus on senior executive decision-making. The rational decision-making model is directed toward making decisions that are logically sound through a series of planning steps. Rational or classical decision-making models typically focus on the point of choice decision, suggesting that decision makers utilize the most comprehensive, valid, and reliable evidence (Lounsbury, 2008; Rehak, Adams, & Belanger, 2010).

The naturalistic decision-making model represents how people make decisions in situations that may involve high stakes, time constraints, or other complex issues. Such decision-making is based on observation, study, and description. Naturalistic decision makers often draw from their own experience or rely on intuition to reach a solution that is "good enough" when faced with complex situations (Kalantari, 2010). Understanding this perspective and how heuristics influence the decision making process of senior executive's when they are using a naturalistic or rational decision making approach is important. This study attempts to understand how senior executives use heuristics in their decision making process which may be defined as a gut feeling, an educated guess, or common sense, when selecting senior-level direct reports.

The construct of senior executive selection has generated increased attention during the past decade from academia, vocational organizations, government agencies, and other institutions (Braddock & McPartland, 1986; Embrick, 2011; Fernandez, 1999; Kirschenman & Neckerman, 1991; Royster, 2003; U.S. Department of Labor, 2010). Such decisions can have a significant impact on an organization's employees, executive teams and shareholders. Senior executives are often in line to succeed the CEO or President, and hold a powerful influence on organizational capabilities, work force, and social structure.

Chapter 2 reviewed the literature related to senior executive decision-making in selecting executive-level direct reports, organizational culture and hiring practices, decision-making theory, heuristics, and cognitive bias. Statement of the problem, research question, significance, and definitions of terms were included, as well as assumptions, limitations, and delimitations of the study. Chapter 3, Methods, presents the study's research design and methodology, the research question, selection criteria, sample recruitment, interview protocol, ethical considerations, procedures, and data analysis.

CHAPTER THREE: METHODS

Introduction

This study utilized a qualitative thematic research approach to examine the heuristics used in decision-making by Fortune 1000 senior executives in selecting their senior-level direct reports. This chapter presents the study's research design and methodology, research question, target population and selection criteria, sampling strategies and recruitment, interview protocol, ethical considerations, procedures for data collection and analysis, and issues of validity and reliability, concluding with a chapter summary.

Research Design and Methodology

Quantitative vs. Qualitative Design

Determining an appropriate research method requires understanding the characteristics of the research study (Fraenkel & Wallen, 2006). Quantitative analysis measures variables and relationships; qualitative analysis describes relationships and human experiences (Creswell, 2012). Quantitative research can be narrow and specific compared to qualitative research, which can be broader and more expansive (Creswell, 2007). The quantitative research method analyzes statistical data, compared to qualitative research that analyzes verbal data obtained through the interview process in conjunction with other supporting documents and artifacts (Fetterman, 2010).

Quantitative research methods are used to explain the relationship of variables associated with an area of interest (Creswell, 2012). A quantitative research study that primarily deals with statistics may include descriptive or comparisons between two or more variables and assumes a potential outcome from the data (Gay, 1996; Neill,

2007). The quantitative approach attempts to explain observation but lacks contextual detail (Neill, 2007). A quantitative survey requiring direct responses to specific questions would not be appropriate for this research study, as the focus is on the direct experiences and perspectives of individual participants. The ability to elaborate when answering questions provides participants an opportunity to be more open about their perceptions of factors that influence their decision-making process when selecting senior-level direct reports (Creswell, 2012).

Qualitative research methodology is used to explore trends or interpret information. Focus is on the human experience and participant descriptions of an experience related to a specific topic through discussions with those involved (Creswell, 2003; Moustakas, 1994). Qualitative research methods incorporate the personal skills of the researcher into the research process through the use of inductive logic in analyzing the data to uncover themes (Neill, 2007). The qualitative method provides an opportunity to develop general concepts based on analysis of the data.

Various configurations were considered when deciding on the research design for this study. For example, the case study examines a common set of traits and characteristics of participants in a specific time period (Creswell, 2012; Neuman, 2006). To understand how senior executives use heuristics in their decision-making process for selecting senior-level direct reports, their perception of the situation must first be known (Fetterman, 2010). Unlike case studies that reveal a connection between the behaviors of an individual that could be controlled by environmental factors (Neuman, 2006), using a qualitative thematic approach can expose detailed information about the perceptions of individuals sharing a culture or behavior (Creswell, 2012). The phenomenon is the essential idea in a qualitative research study (Creswell, 2012). Researchers employing phenomenological research can use participant perceptions to gain insight into a problem (Vickers & Parris, 2007). Participants share information about their experiences and factors that affect their decisions. A phenomenological design requires that participants share a behavior but not a culture (Fetterman, 2010).

In a qualitative study, a researcher should determine the importance of the problem and who benefits from the discoveries (Creswell, 2007, 2012). In addition, the problem to be examined can influence the outcome of specified factors or conditions of the study (Fetterman, 2010). A qualitative research method is more appropriate when making nonspecific examination and gathering data based on perceptions, shared patterns of behavior, and beliefs (Creswell, 2012, p. 21). This study is focused on the perceptions of Fortune 1000 senior executives in describing their decision-making process for selecting senior-level direct reports. Participant responses may provide insight into how heuristics influence those decisions. Organizations may benefit from the findings, as the experiences of these senior executives will shed light on how they describe their decision-making process—with successful or less successful outcomes—in selecting direct reports. Senior executives may benefit through increased understanding of the components of their own decision-making process and the importance they place on each. Further, senior executives may benefit by understanding how individual heuristics can influence their decision-making process for selecting senior-level direct reports.

Research Question

Much of the research in the area of decision-making in an organizational setting has dealt with individuals who are not at a senior executive level (Kerr, Kramer, &

MacCoun, 1996). This study explores the following research question:

> How do senior executives use heuristics during their decision-making process for selecting senior-level executives as their direct reports?

Using a qualitative approach when interviewing senior executives to obtain their perceptions of factors that influenced their decision-making process for selecting senior-level direct reports may identify indicators to improve their decision-making process.

Target Population and Selection Criteria

The population in this study consisted of senior executives of U.S. Fortune 1000 companies. Selection criteria for the specific population group analyzed in this study were the following:

1. Senior executives defined as senior vice president (VP), executive VP, chief executive officer, chief financial officer, chief operating officer, chief human resources officer, chief information officer, and so on.

2. Participants must currently hold the above position or have held the position from 2007 to the present timeframe.

3. Participants must have been responsible for making the final decision to hire a direct report during their time in one of these senior executive roles.

Sampling Strategies and Recruitment

The purposive sampling method was used to recruit 13 study participants. *Purposive sampling* provides a means to reach a targeted group quickly and is useful when there is a specific reason for the research (Cone & Foster, 2006; Creswell, 2012). To locate the participants, I used my database from an executive recruiting business that lists many of the Fortune 1000 senior executives in the retail industry. Previous colleagues, the Linkedin business source, and the Onesource business source were also utilized, as today's senior executives may be more technically knowledgeable than in years past and more receptive to this type of communication (Mamaghani, 2006).

The subcategory of purposive sampling used for this study was *snowball sampling* (Creswell, 2012). Snowball sampling occurs when someone meeting the research criteria is approached about participating in the study and is asked to recommend or refer others who also meet the criteria. Snowball sampling can be useful when the research population is difficult to locate or contact. Participants for this study were recruited through friends, personal database, and social networks.

Telephone and email contacts were made to potential participants in advance to explain the purpose for the study and determine their willingness to participate (Appendix A). After potential participants agreed to be part of the study, a date was set to meet face-to-face or by phone to discuss the confidentiality agreement and to conduct and record the interview. Twelve interviews were conducted by phone and one was completed in a face-to-face interview.

Interview Protocol

The data collection instrument used for this qualitative study consisted of a brief interview protocol of two semi-structured questions (see Appendix D) derived from the study's research question: How do senior executives use heuristics during their decision making process for selecting senior-level direct reports? The critical incident method (Cable & Judge, 1997) was used as a framework for the protocol. For example, each participant was asked to recall a senior-level hiring event that was successful and a senior-level hiring event that proved to be unsuccessful. Critical incident reporting has been found to be effective in qualitative research because participants may offer more specificity versus broad generalizations when answering the questions.

Descriptive research questions are designed to enable understanding of how variables relate and interact with an experience (Neuman, 2006). The semi-structured questions that guided this study were descriptive. The interview questions were designed by the researcher to focus on how senior executives describe their decision-making process for selecting senior-level executives as their senior-level direct reports. In addition, it was anticipated that the perspective and experiences of these senior executives might explain the characteristics they seek in direct reports. Further, it was anticipated that the research would identify individual heuristics used by the senior executives in their decision-making process and highlight the importance placed on each.

Ethical Considerations

Informed Consent

Protecting the rights, values, and integrity of participants while in search of accurate accounts of lived experiences is essential in qualitative research (Creswell, 2012). Accordingly, this research followed the guidelines set forth by the U.S. Department of Health, Education, and Welfare for the protection of human subjects of research. The Interview Protocol for this study and application to conduct research was submitted to, and approved, by the Institutional Review Board of Fielding Graduate University.

Each participant was sent a form letter and a letter of consent prior to taking part in the study (see Appendices A & F). The form letter included information that explained the purpose of the research and provided information about the interview process and approximate time needed to complete the interview. Participants were reminded in the letter that participation is voluntary and that they may elect to withdraw from the study at any time without penalty. The informed consent form included a description of possible benefits to the participant through taking part in the study as well as any foreseeable risks or discomfort that may arise, and a statement describing confidentiality of the records including the data retention period (Appendix F). All participants were given the researcher's contact information in order to discuss their involvement or to ask any questions that may arise from the study.

Participants were required to sign the consent form agreeing to the terms outlined in the document prior to being interviewed; electronic confirmation by email was acceptable. By signing the informed consent, participants confirmed their voluntary participation in the study and their right to renounce their consent to participate at any time (Creswell, 2012).

Confidentiality

The identity of all participants in this study will remain confidential. The researcher conducted twelve interviews by telephone and one in person to collect the data for the study. All research data, including informed consent forms, transcripts from interviews, notes, audiotapes, observational records, reflective notes, data analysis, and electronic files are kept in a locked safe in the researcher's home and will be retained there for at least 3 years from the dissertation approval date. All materials will be destroyed at the end of the 3-year holding period unless the requirement for holding the information changes. The materials will be destroyed according to methods for destroying personal information to include cross-shredding paper materials and erasing, overwriting, or physically destroying any electronic media.

Procedures

Once the prospective study participants were identified, an introductory letter and invitation was sent to the participants via e-mail, as noted above. If participants did not respond to the introductory e-mail after one week, a follow-up e-mail was sent, followed by a phone call (Appendix B). Those respondents who accepted the invitation to participate receive an e-mailed copy of the informed consent form for their review and signature.

Pilot Study

Prior to beginning the main study, a pilot study was conducted with three participants to test the logic and effectiveness of the interview protocol questions and to collect information for the main study. The interview protocol questions were adjusted from 26 to two core questions to facilitate a more open discussion and to allow for more detailed responses from the participants (Appendix D). The pilot study participants were current Fortune 1000 corporate senior executives or those who held the position between 2007 and the present as noted in the study's criteria to participate. Procedures for the pilot study followed those described below for the main study.

Data Collection

Prior to the interview, the participants signed a form agreeing to the terms outlined in the informed consent document (see Appendix F). The researcher administered the interview protocol during one 60-minute phone interview with each participant (see Appendix D). All interviews were audiotaped with a Sony MP3 digital recorder, and reflective notes were taken by the researcher and incorporated into the data analysis where appropriate during the analysis process.

The participants responded to the questions from the interviewer based upon their perception and experiences. While all participants were asked the same brief interview questions, they were free to discuss in detail any observations in the construct that they felt were relevant or important.

A transcriptionist, not connected with the research project, transcribed the interviews verbatim from the audiotapes. Prior to receiving the audiotapes for transcription, the transcriber signed an agreement of confidentiality (see Appendix E). Identifying information for the participants was removed before the participant interviews were given to the transcriptionist.

The participants had an opportunity to verify the accuracy of the transcripts by reviewing their interview transcript post interview. One participant accepted and his assistant confirmed that the participant approved the transcript.

The appropriate sample size for a study is determined through saturation (Creswell, 2012; Newman, 2006). Expansion of the sample size should continue until no new or relevant findings occur. My study consisted of 13 participants. After the sixth interview, the participants introduced no new data pertaining to heuristics or bias, thus the study results reached saturation.

Data Analysis

Qualitative analysis is a methodical process. Using qualitative methods to analyze information requires looking at the problem from a broad perspective and breaking down the information into groups of related data (Creswell, 2007, 2012). The data from transcripts were converted to MS Word documents and imported to the data management software program Atlas.ti 6.2 to organize and identify themes from the perceptions of senior executives of Fortune 1000 organizations in describing their decision-making process when selecting senior-level direct reports.

Themes and Coding

The coding of the data began with the interview transcription and reflective notes using coding methods suggested by the literature (Saldana, 2009). The following is a basic outline of the content analysis methodology used for this study.

Manual coding.

To identify early and emerging concepts and themes the transcripts were examined for individual thoughts, ideas, metaphors, and meanings. During the pre-coding phase the researcher highlighted and underlined important comparative quotes from the participants for analyses and consideration prior to introducing the MS Word document to the Atlas.ti 6.2 data management software program (Saldana, 2009).

The subjective process of constructing qualitative codes is intended to highlight and capture the primary components of the research story that, when organized by similarities, can identify categories and ultimately meaningful connections (Saldana, 2009). Themes were identified and codified based on the significance to the research question: How do senior executives use heuristics during their decision-making process for selecting senior-level direct reports? During the first cycle manual coding process the researcher grouped words and phrases into families with shared characteristics in an effort to understand the purpose of the patterns (Saldana, 2009). For example, the researcher coded words and phrases such as strategic thinker, smart, thinking outside the box, creative, and developed something new as smart/strategic.

Auerbach and Silverstein (as cited in Saldana, 2009) recommended that a visual of the research questions, objectives of the study, theoretical framework, and any other concerns regarding the study be maintained in front of the researcher to focus on the coding process (p. 18). Thus, the researcher referred to the following structured questions as well as 10 prevalent heuristics, their definitions, and use (see Table 1):

- How are leaders saying that they assess and select new leaders?
- What heuristics are they using?
- What assumptions are they making?
- What elements of the hiring process are they citing?
- How do leaders talk about, characterize, and understand what is going on during the interview process?
- What do I see going on in the transcripts and my notes that are consistent themes?
- What should I include in my notes?
- What strikes me?

The first-cycle coding process continued with the selection of words or phrases that linked to the research question. On each participant's transcript, the researcher highlighted words and phrases that related to the heuristics identified previously. For example, the researcher assigned words and phrases associated with cultural fit or personality fit to representative heuristics and confirmation bias when the participants' responses indicated that they were attempting to confirm that the senior-level executive candidate represented their perception of a cultural fit for their organization. As each transcript was reviewed an additional three times, the researcher coded words and phrases with similar meaning which became categories. The categories were matched to the most closely related of the 10 predetermined heuristics (Saldana, 2009, p. 13). For example, the statement "but I knew she fit in culturally based on my experience with her" was assigned to the representative heuristic category because this response from participant 3 indicated his salient belief that the candidate he was interviewing represented the culture of his organization. (See Appendix G: Categories and Heuristics Relationship for the initial assignment of categories and heuristics relationships. The categories derived from the codes are in column 1 and the primary heuristics identified by the researcher as being associated with the participants' words or phrases which became categories are identified in columns 2-4.)

Grouping similar words and phrases according to the number of times they appeared in participants' manuscripts began the coding process. Multiple reviews of the transcripts led to category and subcategory headings established through a blend of in vivo, heuristic, and values coding (Saldana, 2009, p. 51). To augment and confirm the codes established from the manual coding process, the researcher used Atlas.ti 6.2, a computer-assisted qualitative data analysis program, following the procedural steps noted below.

Procedures.

Step 1: Identifying and naming concepts.

As a foundation for data analysis, the researcher began with 10 of the most commonly used and most researched heuristics that could potentially be employed by senior executives during the interviewing process to select senior-level direct reports (see Table 1). From their review of the current decision-making literature and bias literature, Rehak et al. (2010) determined that the majority of heuristics are present in both rational and naturalistic decision-making processes. Their review of the literature suggests that the decision-making process is subject to individual heuristics and biases.

Table 1

Ten Prevalent Heuristics, Their Definitions, and Participant Example

Heuristic	Definition	Participant / Historical Example
Confirmation	The human inclination to see what we expect to see from our environment (Rehak et al., 2010)	"I have them tell me what they like and what they didn't like and what they didn't like about their company…former bosses. And from just listening to that I can tell whether they're going to fit at company X or not." (Participant 10)
Availability	Perceived frequencies of events are affected and subjective probability (Kahneman et al., 1982, p. 164)	"And there's candidates we've interviewed that we thought had lots of talent, but we knew just wouldn't fit inside the organization and would ultimately…wouldn't be effective because they would cause some real damage." (Participant 6)
Representative	The tendency to view a sample drawn from a population as highly representative of that population (Kahneman et al., 1982)	"It also seemed an awful…he also seemed to me to be terribly ego driven and while an interview is a process that kind of lends itself to that, it felt to me that he, more than most, was talking a lot about how good he was and not crediting others." (Participant 7)
Anchoring	When we use a known estimation to judge an unfamiliar event or action (Adams et al., 2009)	"And sometimes you can really test where somebody leans to by making them choose one of two things that are in the extreme that neither they want to do but which would they be most likely to do." (Participant 12)
Overconfidence	The belief that our experiences, knowledge, perceptions of a situation are more correct or positive than they actually are (Adams et al., 2009)	"For whatever reason, we opted not to do that for this role. No so much opted not to do it, didn't even have it as a consideration to do. Primarily, if I'm honest, is because we were so impressed with their background and their pedigree." (Participant 12)

Hindsight	People are more likely to overestimate the outcome of an event when they have prior information than they would have without the information (Rehak et al., 2010)	"I got caught up in a lot of bullshit and I got caught up in a lot of enthusiasm and somebody who was really good at interviewing and somebody who kind of had all the right answers. But the problem was, I didn't ask all the right questions. And so I gave overwhelming support to this person." (Participant 10)
Framing	Humans make decisions based on how problems are framed (Rehak et al., 2010)	None Identified
Affect	We eliminate alternatives by anchoring our decision-making process in a natural starting point (Shah & Oppenheimer, 2008)	"Therefore I saw that unconsciously this guy had become a leader and had accepted a leadership role and the other district managers tended to ask him advice and his opinion. I liked that." (Participant 11)
Satisficing	We apply a modest amount of computations or follow a "rule of thumb" in order to make a decision (Shah & Oppenheimer, 2008)	"You know what happens, in my mind; when you get …when you're in a rush, when you're moving at a speed to hire someone, sometimes you might use a recruiter that is motivated by speed. And when that happens, or when you are having a difficult job to fill, you sometimes will settle for the best…tallest pygmy, as I like to say." (Participant 5)
Statistical	People often fail to use proper statistical reasoning either by ignoring past actualities or focusing on one atypical event to guide their decision or action (Rehak et al., 2010)	"You know what happens, in my mind; when you get …when you're in a rush, when you're moving at a speed to hire someone, sometimes you might use a recruiter that is motivated by speed. And when that happens, or when you are having a difficult job to fill, you sometimes will settle for the best…tallest pygmy, as I like to say." (Participant 5)

Spoken attributions, implicit, inferred, and suggested meanings were explored to reveal the participants' use of heuristics. All key words, expression, thought, and belief were open coded and categorized in order to form concepts. Participant responses to the interview questions were organized based on heuristic association, discussed in detail in Chapter 4, Findings.

Step 2: Atlas.ti 6.2 coding.

The use of the Atlas.ti 6.2 data management software program enhances a qualitative thematic research approach by examining, organizing, and coding the data to reveal commonalities through themes. Themes provide opportunities to define and assess contributing factors to the research problem. The Atlas.ti 6.2 program augmented the thematic approach to this research study and facilitated the grouping process beyond similarities to themes associated with specific heuristics. This computer-assisted qualitative data analysis software allowed the researcher to associate codes across large amounts of data to efficiently organize and reconfigure the data to analyze and interpret the participants' transcripts (Saldana, 2009, p. 22). Atlas.ti software enabled the researcher to view related data in families of codes and categories that are connected to create networks that become themes confirming the most prevalent codes and categories found manually, and their connection to the heuristics used most often by these senior executive participants (see Appendix I).

Step 3: Constant comparison.

The data were reviewed and analyzed several times through Atlas.ti in order to compare each emerging concept with all other concepts. This process involved comparing like responses in order to look for emerging and merging patterns and themes for each response allowing the researcher to codify and categorize the participants' responses with appropriate codes (Saldana, 2009). The researcher participated in two online Atlas.ti training sessions and practiced a total of 7 days prior to uploading the transcripts of the participants' narratives to the Atlas.ti program to discover the nodes that created the family networks.

Codes from the first coding process were manually assigned to categories using the Interview Protocol and the selected heuristics (see Table 1) that served as a conceptual framework for this study as well as highlighting quotes associated with the words identified during the first-cycle coding process. Atlas.ti assisted the researcher in confirming the top recurring codes found manually, the heuristics association, and the most prevalent themes. Atlas.ti confirmed that all of the participants used three of the four most identified heuristics: confirmation bias, representative heuristics, and availability heuristics. Additionally, Atlas.ti confirmed that 12 of the 13 participants used overconfidence bias during their decision-making process for selecting senior-level direct reports.

Step 4: Choosing and situating core categories.

Emerging from the data were five core themes, presented in detail in Chapter 4, Findings. The themes were grouped according to the categories and heuristics they represent. The coding of the data followed the pattern of questions in the interviews and the responses given in order to answer the stated research question. For a detailed breakdown of the coding categories and five core themes, see Appendix H: Coding of Study Results.

Step 5: Assigning heuristics to the emerging themes.

The final step in Atlas.ti was to confirm what heuristics were used, how they were used, and whether the participants use heuristics in a rational or naturalistic decision-making context. As a foundation, I began with 10 of the most used and most researched heuristics that could potentially be employed by senior executives during the interviewing process to select senior-level direct reports: (a) confirmation bias, (b) availability heuristics, (c) representative heuristics, (d) hindsight bias, (e) overconfidence bias, (f) anchoring bias, (g) *satisficing* bias, (h) recognition bias, (i) affect bias, and (j) framing bias (see Table 1). Confirmation bias, availability heuristics, and representative heuristics emerged as being consistently used during the participants' rational and naturalistic decision-making process. Satisficing bias, overconfidence bias, and anchoring bias emerged as being occasionally used by these senior executives. Emerging themes from the data applicable to both rational and naturalistic decision-making methodology were grouped into five core categories. The thematic coding of the data was derived from the two core questions from the Interview Protocol and the participants' responses that answered the overarching research question. Coding categories are detailed in Appendix H: Coding of Study Results.

Issues of Validity and Reliability

A qualitative researcher's main focus is to portray an accurate, honest, and equitable assessment of the "social experiences" of participants in a study (Creswell, 2012). Validity can determine the accuracy of interpretations in a study by establishing if the study measured what the study was supposed to measure (Popham, 2005). Reliability determines that the data collected are consistent and dependable.

Internal Validity

Internal validity refers to the quality and accuracy of a study (Neuman, 2006). Qualitative researchers focus more on accurately portraying the lived experiences of the participants and are less concerned with outcomes related to empirical data (Popham,

2005). Preconceived beliefs concerning the study problem were acknowledged and the researcher was mindful to put those misconceptions and beliefs aside to avoid bias. The initial pilot study tested and further developed the interview protocol (Creswell, 2007, 2012). The use of semi-structured questions in the data collection process allowed the participants to elaborate on their own thought process strengthening the trustworthiness of their responses. The data collection process was monitored continuously by the researcher to reduce errors and validate that research procedures were followed (Cone & Foster, 2006). Audiotaping the interviews ensured that the data accurately reflected the participants' responses.

External Validity

External validity refers to the extent to which the results of the research study can be generalized or used with another population or in another geographic area (Creswell, 2007). These research findings could be used for a similar population in a different geographical area and could also be used for senior-level executives in the targeted population. The findings are based on senior executive perceptions of their decision-making process when selecting senior-level executives as their direct reports. Thus, they are not generalizable to another population.

Reliability

Reliability determines the consistency in measurement of the data (Creswell, 2007). Reliability must be present to determine the validity of a perception (Neuman, 2006). If reliability exists, other researchers using the same data can conduct the research study with comparable results (Creswell, 2007, 2012). Reliability means the data collected is trustworthy and constant over time and across settings (Cone & Foster, 2006).

With qualitative research, the focus is not on measuring data but on finding information about behaviors, perceptions, and values (Creswell, 2007). The validity of the study was strengthened because the population represented Fortune 1000 senior executives from different corporations.

Chapter Summary

This study utilized a qualitative design to examine the decision-making process of Fortune 1000 senior executives when selecting senior-level executives as direct reports. It was anticipated that participant responses would reveal heuristics utilized by the senior executive participants in the decision-making process. The study sample was recruited through purposive and snowball sampling techniques. Eligible participants met the criteria for the study as current Fortune 1000 senior executives, or those who held that position within the last 5 years, and were responsible for hiring one or more senior-level direct report(s) during that timeframe.

The Interview Protocol, consisting of semi-structured questions, was administered to participants through one 60-minute, audiotaped telephone interview. A transcriptionist unrelated to the project transcribed the interview data. The researcher analyzed the data with the use of the Atlas.ti 6.2 data management software program, in addition to manual coding, to discover themes from participant responses.

The following chapter, Findings, presents participant demographics, a brief overview of heuristics and bias, and a detailed presentation of the common themes and categories resulting from analysis of the data.

CHAPTER FOUR: RESULTS

Introduction

The purpose of this dissertation was to examine how senior executives use heuristics in their decision-making process for selecting senior-level executives as their direct reports. Understanding this process can assist in identifying how they conceptualize the components of, and identify the heuristics that inform their decision-making process. Further, determining the importance that senior executives place on each component of their decision-making process may assist in improving their decision-making in selecting senior-level direct reports.

This chapter presents participant demographics, an overview of bias and heuristics, a review and description of the frequently used heuristics, common themes that emerged from the data, and five core categories that were grouped from the themes, concluding with a chapter summary.

Participants

Nineteen (19) potential participants were initially recruited, however 6 declined to participate in the study. Of those who declined, 3 were not interested and one responded that he could not allow more than 30 minutes to participate. Two were available "if needed," but did not participate in the study. The final sample was comprised of 13 participants.

The study participants included current or senior executives that held the title of senior vice president (VP), executive vice president, chief executive officer, chief operating officer, or chief human resources officer in a Fortune 1000 organization between 2007 and 2012. The participant demographics included two White females, one African

American male, one Latino male, and nine White males. Their position titles included chief executive officer (2), president (3), executive VP (2), senior VP (2), and senior human resources officer (4).

The senior executive participants had between 10 and 15 years experience in senior-level executive positions and 5+ years as C-suite, or highest-level executives. All participants indicated that they had hired over 20 senior-level executives. All participants were employed at national and global retail chains with the exception of one employed at a global human resource organization and one employed at a global hotel chain. The following brief profiles provide individual background information as to current and/or past executive-level position and employer as well as number of direct reports and their titles.

Participant Profiles

Participant 1.

Gregg previously held the position of president of a $40 billion Fortune 500 retail organization with 125,000 employees and 6,100 outlets. Most recently he was the CEO and president of a $7 billion retail organization with outlets throughout the world. The number of Gregg's senior-level direct reports fluctuated generally between 6-12 with the titles of vice president, senior vice president, and executive senior vice president.

Participant 2.

Kathy was the executive senior vice president of human resources for a $36 billion retail food chain with 100,000 employees located primarily in North America. Kathy had 13 direct reports that held the title of vice president or senior vice president.

Participant 3.

Louis was recently the president of a $42 billion retail organization based in the Midwest. The organization has 293,000 employees and 6,300 outlets or families. Louis had 25 direct reports with the titles of chief merchandising officer, executive senior vice president, and vice presidents of various divisions and functional areas.

Participant 4.

Robb is currently the chief human resource officer for a $4 billion worldwide hotel chain based in the Midwest. The organization has 50,000 employees and over 400 units. Robb has six direct reports with the titles of senior vice president, vice president, and director. Previously, Robb was the chief human resource officer for a $200 billion organization based in New York City.

Participant 5.

Larry is currently the senior vice president – president and business unit general manager for a $19 billion food manufacturing and retail organization based in Texas. The organization has 19,000 employees. Larry's number of direct reports fluctuates, but he currently has eight with the title of vice president or director.

Participant 6.

Dave is currently the executive senior vice president and chief human resources officer for a $40 billion retail food and drug organization based in the Midwest with locations throughout America. Dave has six direct reports and 16 indirect reports.

Participant 7.

Karen was recently the executive senior vice president and chief human resource officer for a $13 billion food manufacturing and consulting organization based in the Midwest with offices throughout the world. The organization has 9,000 employees. She is currently a human resource consultant for the organization and has seven direct reports with the titles of vice president or director.

Participant 8.

Rick was recently the executive senior vice president of merchandising and marketing for a $70 billion retail organization with 365,000 employees and 1,875 companies throughout America and Canada. Rick averaged eight direct reports with the titles of senior vice president, vice president, and director.

Participant 9.

Mike is the former president and chief operating officer for a $40 billion food and drug retail operation based in the Midwest. The organization has 125,000 employees. The number of Mike's direct reports fluctuated between six and ten with the titles of executive senior vice president, senior vice president, and vice president.

Participant 10.

Pete was recently the executive senior vice president of operations for a $36 billion food and drug operation located in the Midwest. The organization has 100,000 employees and Pete had nine senior-level direct reports that held the titles of division president, senior vice president, and vice president.

Participant 11.

Terry was the senior vice president with a retail organization currently based out of Canada. The organization has 6,000 employees and Terry's 13 direct reports included vice presidents, directors, and district managers.

Participant 12.

Keith is currently the president of a $6 billion division of a $40 billion food and drug retail operation. Keith's division has 25,000 employees and he has seven direct reports with the titles of vice president or director.

Participant 13.

John is the president and chief officer of one of the largest outplacement firms (private) in the world with offices throughout America, Canada, and Europe. John's direct reports have titles that include executive senior vice president, senior vice president, and vice president.

Bias and Heuristics Overview

Because the words *bias* and *heuristics* are often used concurrently it is important to understand the meaning of each, and it is important to know how heuristics are manifested into biases that cause errors in judgment (Adams, Rehak, Brown, & Hall, 2009).

Bias can be defined as "an inclination of temperament or outlook; *especially* : a personal and sometimes unreasoned judgment" (Merriam-Webster, 2012a, sec. 3b). Bias can be a "systematic error introduced into sampling or testing by selecting or encouraging one outcome or answer over others" (sec. 3d2). Seminal research by Tversky and Kahneman (1974) showed that human decision-making biases are present because humans are incapable of making optimal decisions in all situations. Accordingly, humans take shortcuts and often apply a rule of thumb seeking a satisfactory solution using heuristics. Reliance on heuristics helps us to make satisfactory decisions and perform efficiently. However, reliance on heuristics can also cause predictable and systematic errors (Adams, et al., 2010). This research has identified some of the heuristics that senior executives use when they are selecting senior-level executives as their direct reports.

Findings

As noted in Chapter 3, as a foundation for data analysis, I began with 10 of the most widely used and researched heuristics that could potentially be employed by senior executives during the interviewing process: (a) confirmation bias, (b) availability heuristics, (c) representative heuristics, (d) hindsight bias, (e) overconfidence bias, (f) anchoring bias, (g) *satisficing* bias, (h) recognition bias, (i) affect bias, and (j) framing bias (see Table 1).

Data analysis revealed that 7 of the 10 were used by the senior executive participants in their decision-making process for selecting senior executive direct reports: (a) confirmation bias, (b) availability heuristics, (c) representative heuristics, (d) anchoring bias, (e) overconfidence bias, (f) affect bias, and (g) satisficing bias. Three of these were used minimally: (a) anchoring (5 times); (b) affect (9 times); and (c) satisficing (4 times). The remaining 4 of the 7 heuristics used by the senior executive participants (confirmation, availability, representative, overconfidence) are addressed below in the presentation of the five core categories discovered in the analysis of the data.

Common Themes

Five general themes emerged from the findings during data analysis:

1. Senior executives use both a rational and naturalistic decision-making approach for selecting senior-level direct reports, and they use heuristics during both processes.

2. Senior executives believe that a cultural fit is critical to the success of executives in their organization, but they could not explicitly define their organization's culture. Thus, they use a naturalistic decision-making

approach and they apply heuristics during the decision-making process to determine the cultural fit of a potential new senior-level direct report.

3. Senior executives use heuristics during their naturalistic decision-making process to determine personality fit and leadership style.

4. Senior executives follow a rational decision-making approach when evaluating the experience, previous contributions, and education of potential senior-level direct reports, and they apply heuristics.

5. Senior executives are overconfident of their decision-making process for selecting successful senior-level direct reports for their organization and they apply heuristics.

These themes are discussed in greater detail below in the descriptions of the five core categories that emerged from the research.

Five Core Categories

Using a qualitative thematic research approach, and through content analysis using Atlas.ti 6.2 data management software, five core categories were determined from the above themes that emerged from the research data. These five core categories will address the research question on how senior executives use heuristics during their decision-making process for selecting senior-level executives as direct reports.

Core Category 1: Rational and Naturalistic Decision-Making.

In order to begin the conceptualization of which decision-making approach senior executives followed, and to obtain data to analyze how each participant uses heuristics in their decision-making process, the researcher asked all participants the same two core questions: (a) to describe a successful hiring event and (b) to describe a hiring event that was unsuccessful (see Appendix D, for Interview Protocol). Participants were asked to elaborate on their thought process, how they assessed and evaluated the candidates, what ultimately determined their decision to hire the executive-level candidate, and their thoughts on the positive or negative outcome. In all cases, the senior executives used a rational approach to their decision-making process when reviewing the candidate's work experience and previous contributions, and a naturalistic decision-making approach when vetting each candidate for cultural fit, personality fit, and leadership style.

Rational decision-making approach.

Senior executive participants' rational application was connected directly with the candidate's work experience and accomplishments that included review of resumes, application, reference checks, and psychological evaluations. Participant 2 used a rational decision-making approach, explaining, "so this person had a lot of Wall Street experience and kind of had a pretty big personality, but was very smart in areas" (Interview database line 110; henceforth noted as "ll"). Similarly, Participant 11 was impressed by the candidate's documented past achievements: "This individual had sterling reviews over the years, had received consistent raises, in the highest percentile, as well, had achieved his region's performance awards" (ll. 077). Participant 6, as well, emphasized the candidate's performance history in making the final hiring decision: "We liked him a lot based on his history of accomplishments, everything he has done, and made the hire" (ll. 029). Participant 3 summed up his rational decision-making process: "Well, if I am looking at all the data, the results and the opinion survey and upward leadership feedback, and I am talking to people, I have a pretty good sense for how they have driven those results" (ll. 47).

Each participant indicated that he or she assumed that the individual met the qualifications but also wanted to personally confirm them. Participant 4 expressed his thoughts about the priorities of others involved in the interviewing process: "I got the feeling that they were really, really interviewing for content, the experience--tell me, you know, what you have done." This caused the participant concern regarding what was most important: confirming results or intuitively confirming cultural and personality fit? (ll. 68-69).

Naturalistic decision-making approach.

Each of the senior executives used an intuitive, naturalistic approach during their final decision-making process to ensure that the candidate was a cultural and personality fit for their team. In one example, Participant 3 explained, "but I felt the other guy was stronger and would fit into the culture better if he was just like a New York tough guy."

Participant 4 acknowledged using an intuitive approach regarding personality fit in selecting a senior-level direct report:

> Well by virtue of the fact that I know this guy in New York really well and he said, I'll vouch for this guy. He's a great guy, let me introduce you to him. That's already, you know, that already takes dating to the next level. Now, it's a friend of a friend so I'm feeling a little more comfortable that I'm not making a bad decision. And he lives in Chicago, so--and he's Canadian and I'm Canadian. (ll. 072)

The importance of personality fit was noted by Participant 5 in describing what he looks for in a senior-level candidate: "So someone who I believe is going to have that cultural fit--not so much, I guess organizationally, but with me personally." Here the participant used a naturalistic decision-making approach and applied heuristics.

Other participants also noted the importance of fitting into the organization's culture. Participant 4 described his organizational environment: "I think that there is a great sense of caring for each other, it kind of feels very family-like here" (ll. 38). Similarly, Participant 2 expressed, "They've got to really understand the culture of the company and they've got to understand the interaction of the CEO and they've got to understand the executive team, because really what you're doing when you're trying to put a team together is kind of like building a family" (ll. 026).

When asked to describe the organizational culture, Participant 3 moved from a rational perspective to a naturalistic approach to his decision-making process:

> Once you can put aside, look, you are obviously capable based on your education and your background and your achievements, the next component becomes, is it a fit here? Can they work with the people that are here and add some value by bringing everyone else up to a level that we want to be at? That becomes more intuitive. (ll. 68-69)

Core Category 2: Organization Culture and Heuristics.

The core questions asked by the researcher revealed consistency in the responses from all participants about the importance of a cultural fit and confirmed that each participant used a naturalistic approach when speaking about a cultural fit. The most frequently stated general definition of cultural fit included the candidate's leadership style, ability to collaborate, team builder, positive attitude, strong desire to be on the team, and ability to communicate at all levels. However, when the researcher probed deeper asking the participants to describe cultural fit there were inconsistencies in their responses further confirming their naturalistic approach to the cultural fit construct. Below is a representation of the senior executives' responses when describing the general definition of cultural fit. Their responses indicate the indefinable nature of this construct and illustrate the use of a naturalistic decision-making approach as defined earlier and the use of confirmation bias, representative heuristics, and availability heuristics when assessing senior-level executive candidates for a cultural fit with their organization.

Confirmation bias and cultural fit.

All of the participants showed evidence of confirmation bias in their response to the two core questions. Their responses showed similarities with many of the terms and statements used when representing confirmation bias (Shah & Oppenheimer, 2008; Adams et al., 2009).

Participant 4 held a vivid picture of the behavior that he was seeking for his new senior-level direct report, although he was not explicit in his response to his supervisor when he explained that he wanted to hire someone other than the individual his supervisor recommended. He was seeking to confirm his intuition that a candidate that displayed excitement deserved the position more than other candidates:

> And when I was setting [sic] down talking to my boss about where I was coming out on it, he said, well what about this person? And I said you know, she doesn't, I don't think she deserves to work here. And I think this is a fabulous opportunity. It's a fabulous company, and if somebody isn't excited about it now, then they should maybe go someplace else. And this guy was excited. I mean the one I hired. You could tell he was, you could tell by the questions he asked. He was just engaged. He wasn't going through the motion. (ll. 046-047)

This naturalistic decision-making approach caused the participant to turn down one candidate, though others believed that she was the right person for the position. This allowed the senior executive the opportunity to teach others in the organization the importance of hiring individuals that are excited about working for the organization, reaffirming his belief that the demonstration of excitement by senior-level executive candidates during the interview process is a characteristic that confirms the candidate's cultural fit for his organization.

A variety of leadership competencies were described to support the participants' confirmation bias when determining cultural fit, such as the need to be collaborative, confirming that the candidate's ego was not an issue, positive attitude, shared personality, professionalism, Ivy League education, strong desire, being smart, strategic thinker, thinking outside the box, and values match. In no case did these senior executives indicate that the competencies they were confirming were in writing and were a formal part of the executive selection process.

The researcher asked Participant 9 to explain a previous statement he made regarding a senior-level executive's cultural fit for his organization. Participant 9 offered no task-specific examples and used intuition and confirmation bias during his naturalistic decision-making process to determine the cultural fit of the candidate:

> I think one of the best ways to do that, Roy, that I found is to have them meet some people at different levels of the organization. So all the way from two or three levels below where they're going to be peers to then a level above or two levels above, a broad range of people. And not ask those people to interview him, just say, this is someone we're thinking about bringing into the organization. (ll. 063-065)

This allowed the senior executive to confirm his intuition that the candidate was a good cultural fit prior to making the final offer. Participant 9 used confirmation bias when he explained the meaning of a previous statement the researcher asked him to explain, suggesting that the senior-level candidates he hired were strategic thinkers:

> It's really the ability in our industry to think outside the box. To really take things, take information, take events, pull them together, draw some new conclusion and develop something new, something that hasn't been. Breaking new ground, I call it, thinking outside the box, taking the organization in a different direction, and because of certain events, and thinking longer term. Not acting tactically, acting with vision. Being able to conceptualize things the way they should be or could be or going to be. Articulate that to the organization and then mobilize the organization to pursue that. (ll. 053-055)

This response confirms that Participant 9 was analyzing the candidate intuitively and using confirmation bias in attempting to confirm the candidate's ability to perform the job based on previous beliefs and expectations about other people that he perceived as being successful.

Participants represented confirmation bias during their naturalistic decision-making process in connection with cultural fit for senior-level candidates most often by interjecting words such as *family* to explain their intuitive decision-making process. These participants' responses suggest that they believe hiring a senior-level direct report that appeared to represent the characteristics of a family member was a cultural fit and good for the organization. Thus, it was their duty to hire senior-level direct reports that represented a family member.

Participant 4 was excited to explain his meaning of cultural fit, exclaiming,

> The culture is, I think there's great pride in, in the, I think servant leadership plays --we would never call it that. But I think it's a hospitality company so we're very others oriented. Humility is massive. I think because the people, the family who, who founded the company, if I had to pick one core value to their family, I would say humility. (ll. 036)

Participant 2 was deeply invested in ensuring that senior-level executive candidates were not only a cultural fit but also that they embraced the culture as a family member. This senior executive's high level of motivation to support the salient belief that a cultural fit should represent a family member was paramount for the organization. She supported her naturalistic decision-making process using confirmation bias, stating,

> They've got to really understand the culture of the company and they've got to understand the interaction of the CEO and they've got to understand the executive team, because really what you're doing when you are trying to put a team together is kind of like building a family and so you've got to make sure that by the time candidates are presented to somebody like in my position, they already know the nuts and bolts and of the tactical pieces of the work. You are really hiring for personality fit, ethics, integrity, those kinds of things and so it's very different than, you know, making sure a person knows the law. (ll. 102-027)

Another key characteristic that all the participants identified, using a naturalistic decision-making process and confirmation bias to determine the candidate's cultural fit was collaboration. Participant 7 used her salient beliefs to confirm the cultural and personality fit for a senior-level executive candidate. The responses of this participant revealed her objective to satisfy her intuitive preference to select direct reports based on her perception of their level of collaboration.

> It's starting to sound like a theme; we're not that superficial here. But he had an impressive business background, his McKinsey background and some of the big accounts he'd worked. So those things, plus his approach to being collaborative, are the kinds of things that made me think he would fit. (ll. 204-206)

Use of representative heuristics.

Adams et al. (2009) suggest that representative heuristics allows people to make a simple similarity judgment, thereby reducing time and effort. This might lead to errors in judgment and biased decisions (p. 12). Factors that promote representative heuristics include time pressure, class similarity, cognitive comfort, and decision-making overconfidence.

All of the participants used representative heuristics in their answers to the core question, expressing that a cultural and personality fit were paramount to the success of a new senior-level direct report. These senior executives could not explicitly define their perception of what specific characteristics or values a candidate would express during the interview, but were comfortable with their intuitive understanding of the attributes that would confirm the candidate's cultural fit. The participants used representative heuristics to assess whether the executive-level candidate fit into the parent population that represented a cultural fit for their organization. Participant 4 spoke of the importance of engaging candidates in different situations when looking for cultural fit:

> And people are complex, human beings are complex. Some people take tests well. Some people interview well. Which is why you're really, an old friend of mine said before you hire somebody for a really senior position, see them in three different settings. See them, you know, in your office. See them, I don't know, at dinner and then see them, go play a round of golf with them. I think the latter, I think the round of golf is the most telling. (ll. 68-69)

This participant had salient beliefs that he accessed using representative heuristics during these events to confirm or deny the senior-level executive's cultural fit within his organization.

Another participant used representative heuristics, offering a vivid depiction of the candidate he preferred and showing why he believed that a "New York tough guy" would be successful:

> The hiring process was the standard outside recruiter. Anyway, and then he brought in his stacks of resumes and we basically, myself and the current, and the existing financial team, which was really at the time one level down from the CFO, picked one person. And the founder and the private equity company picked this guy, the coach guy, which I was okay with. But I felt the other guy was stronger and would fit into the culture better if he was just like a New York tough guy. The guy was slick, kind of preppy Connecticut guy with an unbelievable education. I mean background, Harvard MBA, all that kind of stuff. So we had a lot of

discussion. And this guy came out on top based on just a voting thing. And he lasted about 90 days. (Participant 3, ll. 62-63)

During the interview, Participant 6 used representative heuristics to assess desired characteristics during the naturalistic decision-making process for selecting a senior-level direct report. Participant 6 responded to the researcher's follow-up question to explain cultural fit:

> It's a combination of things, and part of it is the compassion part, how they dealt with people. Part of it is their passion for the business and how much they love the retail business, and that's an important piece. Part of it is what's their ego display like? Do they require lots of attention? Are they people who, for whom visible displays of status are important? And if they are, they're not going to be a good fit here. What's their receptivity to working collaboratively with others as opposed to having to be the one who is always right? Those are some of the cultural components that's [sic] important to company X. (ll. 077-079)

Participant 10 described cultural fit at his organization using representative heuristics:

> So cultural fit at X company would be a couple things. One, even though we work in unique functional areas, at company X we communicate cross-functionally, right? You let other functional areas know what's going on in your area. Well that's not how X thought about things. X just thought he had to live in his own little sanctum and do his own little thing, and that's just how he thought . . . that's just how he worked. Well it created massive problems because his department stretched across other departments, especially retail. (ll. 091)

In response to a direct follow-up question as to whether structured or specific questions were in place to ask senior-level candidates in assessing their cultural fit with the organization, the participants revealed that no such procedures were available. Thus, they accessed representative heuristics during their naturalistic decision-making process for selecting direct reports. Participant 6 elaborated,

> Now I always start . . . my own style, I always start with having them talk about their experience, and I obviously read all the information we had on them ahead of time. And then I use that to probe into specific examples from their experience. So I ground . . . All my questions are based on, "tell me how you handled this or tell

me about a time you had to deal with a change process. Tell me about a time you had to introduce innovation into the organization." (ll. 083-085)

Participant 10 believed that he could find the perfect cultural fit if he had the candidates give specific examples in each of their responses. Based on the responses of the senior-level executive, Participant 10 demonstrated that he could access the appropriate representative heuristics for consideration:

> I'll start with leadership. So what does it mean . . . to be more specific, what are the components I am looking for in a leader? What I want to hear is I want examples, tough examples, where this individual influenced people to follow. Because that to me is the one-sentence definition of a leader, is that they have followers that want to be following somebody, and so give me examples of that. So I'll ask . . . I'll say to them, give me an example of the toughest thing you ever had to lead. How many people did you have to influence? How many people had to come with you? How did you do it? What were the obstacles you hit? Tell me a story about that. (ll. 051-055).

Other participants revealed their use of representative heuristics during their naturalistic decision-making process in their effort to match the senior-level executive candidate with the culture of their organization. One participant exclaimed, "One, from a demographic standpoint was he old enough to have been successful but young enough to connect, because the workforce was a very young workforce." (Participant 12, ll. 079) Participant 3 wanted a personal connection with the new senior-level direct report, using representative heuristics to support his intuition that the candidate was a personal fit: "So someone who I believe is going to have that cultural fit, not so much I guess organizationally number 1, but number 2 with me personally, that's really the key." (ll. 035)

Use of availability heuristics.

Factors that promote availability heuristics include intuition, subjectivity, limited view, time restrictions, workload, vividness, and salience (Adams et al., 2010).

The data revealed that 12 participants used availability heuristics during their naturalistic decision-making process for selecting a senior-level direct report. These senior executives accessed salient available information intuitively to determine the probability of the cultural fit of a senior-level direct report (Adams et al., 2010; Kahneman et al., 1982). For example, Participant 10 followed a naturalistic decision-making approach using availability heuristics to explain his view of the cultural fit construct: "So even if it's not what is representative of the culture, if there's a culture you're trying to move your company to. And you need to be sure that you're hiring or promoting people that kind of align with that." (ll. 115)

Some participants expressed fear of selecting a senior-level direct report that was not a fit.

> So when the time came, he left, he got a great job. Somebody bought him with a lot of money and stuff. I said, you know what? Go for it. Good for you. I will miss you as an individual, thank you for your contributions. But I've already replaced him with somebody. It took 6 months. But I replaced him with someone. I replaced him with someone I knew. Who I [knew], because I thought, I can't afford to have another failure in this role. Because there's too much at stake. (ll. 66-68)

Others were resolved that a cultural fit was most important for the senior-level candidate's success and the organization's growth. They used available heuristics to support their naturalistic decision-making process in an effort to ensure that they selected a candidate that would be a cultural fit and thus have a higher probability of success in the organization. This suggests that these participants estimated the probability of the senior-level executive candidate's success using similar associations.

> You can kind of align with how we think about it at company X because, especially in the higher ranks, Roy, if there's a mismatch there, nothing else really matters. You can't get past it. People can't perform well, people don't . . . All the other things just kind of go to hell if a person just doesn't fit. (Participant 10, ll. 003-004)

Participant 5, using availability heuristics in the context of success probability, stated,

> The word "culture" which goes back . . . I think it's overused but the word "culture" is really important because not all cultural places where people come from are the same, and flourishing under one type of culture you may not flourish in another, under a different one. So someone who I believe is going to have that cultural fit, not so much. . . . I guess organizational, number 1, but number 2, with me personally. That's really the key. (ll. 35)

However, when Participant 5 was asked directly what cultural fit meant to him, he reflected intuitively on available information and responded,

> So what I am looking for are people that value the contribution of those around them, that don't need to be the one getting all the praise, who willingly give that up in the name of leadership, that reach down and pull the people below them up by making them feel great about success and the wins that they're getting. (ll. 43)

Table 2 depicts the number of specific heuristics used by these participants during their naturalistic decision-making process to determine a cultural fit for potential senior-level direct reports.

Table 2

Participants' Use of Heuristics for Cultural Fit

Heuristics / Bias	No. of Responses re Cultural Fit
Confirmation (rational)	0
Confirmation (naturalistic)	69
Representative (rational)	0
Representative (naturalistic)	66
Availability (rational)	0
Availability (naturalistic)	49

Core Category 3: Personality Fit, Leadership Style, and Heuristics

In response to the researcher's core questions about the elements of their decision-making process for selecting senior-level executives as their direct reports, all of the participants said that personality or leadership style is a key attribute for potential senior-level hires. All participants used a naturalistic approach to make this decision and the researcher identified the use of representative heuristics and confirmation bias during the narratives of their decision-making process.

Kahneman et al. (1982) observed that when an event, process, or class is "highly representative" of another event, process, or class individuals access representative heuristics to judge the degree to which they are similar (p. 4). Conversely, if there are few similarities between events, classes, or processes, individuals use representative heuristics to judge the probability of their association as low (Kahneman, et al., 1982). The following examples illustrate how these participants accessed representative heuristics to assess for personality fit and leadership style during their decision-making process for selecting senior-level direct reports:

Participant 1 used representative heuristics in selecting a successful candidate, noting the importance of familiarity: "You know, part of the success of these hiring decisions I think has a lot to do with familiarity of the candidate, and probably more importantly either, you know, a clear comfort ability to either awareness or involvement" (ll. 017). Similarly, Participant 5 used representative heuristics and confirmation bias, noting the importance of chemistry:

> And there's no doubt in my mind that when you're hiring into a field, you're hiring into a field you are familiar with, that you pretty well can get to the skills, the hard skills, the technical skills, real quickly . . . whether the person has what it takes from a tactical standpoint. That seems to be the easiest thing to qualify or to quantify, both I guess, when you are hiring. So the trick or the piece of it that really makes a difference to me is when I feel this hard thing to put your hands on called chemistry. (ll. 023)

Representative heuristics were used by Participant 4 in his description of "something that clicks" with a candidate. He added, "And it isn't, I mean he and I are not alike, so this wasn't a case of me hiring in my own likeness" (ll. 100).

Personality fit was noted by Participant 2 in her use of representative heuristics and intuitive approach to hiring: "You are really hiring for personality fit, ethics, integrity, those kinds of things and so it's very different, you know, than making sure a person knows the law" (ll. 016).

Participant 3 explained how his team lined up behind a senior-level candidate's leadership style, and the candidate was ultimately hired. Participant 3 used both representative and confirmation bias in the hiring decision, stating,

> I think everyone agreed that the top three candidates were qualified. And then it came down to whom is everyone comfortable with. And it's funny that people that are comfortable with people that kind of mirror their lifestyle or how, I don't know how to put it, and I don't know if it's lifestyle, but people that they're comfortable with. So you can kind of see them all line up for just the person just based on kind of the personality. (ll. 068)

Participant 3 later explained that this individual was not successful.

In another example of an unsuccessful hire, Participant 10 used a naturalistic decision-making approach and representative heuristics when he explained how he made a poor decision to select a senior-level direct report because he was caught up in the candidate's charismatic personality:

> I got caught up in a lot of bullshit and I got caught up in a lot of enthusiasm and somebody who was really good at interviewing and somebody who kind of had all the answers. (ll. 081)
>
> And within 2 months after he came on the job it was clear I'd made a mistake. I had misread this guy and as the year progressed he got worse and worse and ultimately got fired. I reflected back and said, what the hell did I do wrong here? How could I have been so bamboozled by this guy? (Participant 10, ll. 083)

This caused the participant to examine his interviewing approach and to make critical adjustments in an effort to confirm that a senior-level executive candidate represented his vision of personality fit, cultural fit, and leadership style fit. Participant 10 was not aware that he selected this senior-level executive candidate because the candidate was similar to or representative of his perception of previous successful candidates (Adams et al., 2010).

In an example of a candidate who was well liked by the team and had excellent program development qualifications, Participant 7 applied representative heuristics in deciding not to hire:

> Ultimately, I came pretty close to hiring the Company X person because my team loves her to death, but I decided the fit was not right. I don't think she and our customers will fit well. She's a little edgy and our customers are not, and I decided, boy she's wonderful and we love her and she'll be great at developing programs, but the fit with our customers has to be there. (ll. 117)

Core Category 4: Experience, Contributions, Education, and Heuristics

In this category the researcher identified consistencies and inconsistencies in the participants' responses related to selecting senior-level executives based on their work experience, previous contributions, and education. All the participants reported using a rational or naturalistic decision-making approach when confirming the candidate's experience and previous contributions as well as their significant influence on their current employer. However, participants showed varying levels of availability and representativeness heuristics, and confirmation bias in relation to candidates' past experience and contributions. The participants seem to have combined the use of heuristics (e.g., representative and confirmation biases) as well as a rational decision-making process when considering work experience. Surprisingly, the researcher found that although these senior executives use a naturalistic decision-making approach less often when assessing a candidate's experience, they showed evidence of confirmation bias, and seem to have used both representative availability heuristics virtually equally during their naturalistic decision-making process for selecting a senior-level direct report. However, when the senior executives considered the candidate's experience, previous contributions, and education (and the candidate's education was obtained from an Ivy League school), the senior executives seemed to rely on confirmation bias or representative heuristics and focused primarily on the candidate's education. Table 3 depicts the summary findings from the participant interviews in this core category.

Table 3

Participants' Use of Decision-Making Approaches and Applied Heuristics

Heuristics / Bias	No. of Responses re Experience	No. of Responses re Previous Contributions	No. of Responses re Education
Confirmation (Rational and Naturalistic)	35	16	0
Confirmation (Naturalistic only)	13	0	13
Representative (Rational and Naturalistic)	26	13	0
Representative (Naturalistic only)	11	0	11
Availability (Rational and Naturalistic)	0	16	0
Availability (Naturalistic only)	13	0	0

Below is a representation of how some of the participants used heuristics in their decision-making process for selecting senior-level direct reports when considering experience, previous contributions, and education.

Use of availability heuristics.

Participant 6 applied availability heuristics from a rational decision-making perspective, citing the candidate's experience, when he stated, "I think we interviewed a variety of candidates. One of the factors that put this candidate head and shoulders above the others was the fact that he had specific grocery experience" (ll. 045). In this example, then, the availability of the candidate's previous experience served as a guiding heuristic for assessing their competence that may have overridden other possible characteristics that could be equally diagnostic of their probable future performance.

Combining availability heuristics with rational considerations, then, Participant 8 explained his process, "first are just reports and data, things that I can read the material and how the person performed and delivered results, whether it's sales, profit, in stocks. What was their opinion survey? What does their team think of them? What's their upward leadership feedback?" (ll. 020-022). The probability that a senior-level executive would be successful was considered to be high if he or she excelled at the above criteria because that selection process had previously resulted in success.

Use of representative heuristics.

Participant 7 reported using a rational decision-making approach when considering candidates' experience and previous contributions and followed a naturalistic decision-making approach when considering organizational fit. She used representative heuristics to assist in the decision-making process:

> All these candidates were pretty high-powered people, they came from big companies, they had executive roles, and they came with pretty significant track

records. I made this acquisition, I spun off this division, I helped this group develop this product, and you know they came with accomplishments. So it was a little tough to sort out, to understand which . . . given that they all came with big track records, big resumes, it was a little tough to see your way through which of these people would be the best fit for our environment and our task and who would be successful and who wouldn't. (ll. 161-162)

Participant 9 used representative heuristics combined with rational decision-making when he said, "we like him a lot based on his history of accomplishments, everything he had done, and made the hire" (ll. 149). Similarly, Participant 11 combined both rational and naturalistic decision-making approaches (i.e., using representative heuristics) when he stated, "so he had reviews, spotless history, people rated his integrity and character as being at a very high level, and that is, again, what I wanted to be the face of the corporation out in the field" (ll. 091).

Confirmation bias.

Participant 2 had strong opinions about the candidate that she wanted for her senior-level direct report because of long-held beliefs about individuals that she perceived to be successful. Experience was of critical importance. Thus, she seemed to show confirmation bias in her decision-making processes when she stated, "they were either too technical down a rat hole, didn't have broad enough experience or no retail experience, or too highfalutin'" (ll. 058). Conversely, Participant 10's responses indicate that he used confirmation bias during his naturalistic decision-making approach after rationally considering the senior-level executives' experience. In part of his response to the researcher's core question he stated, "but now I reflect a lot more on what did they do with that experience? What influences did they have with others? I ask them to tell me a story about how you handled a certain situation, and that's what I want to hear." (ll. 017). In this case, then, the participant seems to have extended the meaning of experience to confirm his pre-existing beliefs about candidates, such that experience alone was not a wholly adequate indicator of their competence.

Core Category 5: Senior Executive Overconfidence Bias and Heuristics

The interviews provided some initial evidence of possible overconfidence biases among the executives in relation to their hiring. Each senior executive suggested from memory that they have hired or promoted more than 20 executives during the course of their career, and several estimated at least 100, with few direct reports failing. However, when each of the participants described one recent hiring decision that did not go well they all reported following the same interviewing process they had followed previously with a few adjustments to ensure their original process was followed more stringently. All of the participants stated that they learned something from their unsuccessful hiring events. Specifically, unsuccessful hires seemed to reinforce their perception that allowing more time to vet potential senior-level executives specifically for cultural and personality fit would improve their chances of hiring a direct report that would be successful in their organization. The fact that senior executives saw their incorrect hiring decisions as a product of inadequate time rather than possibly the product of problematic decision-making processes may reflect their overconfidence in their skills. Their hiring experience and perceived success in selecting senior-level direct reports may have contributed to their overconfidence (combined with confirmation bias and their use of representative heuristics), when assessing the candidate's cultural fit and personality fit. The data suggest that all of these participants failed to realize that their unsuccessful hiring event was due to their own overconfidence when repeating the same interviewing and hiring approach.

Participants' overconfidence in their ability to select a senior-level direct report (perhaps influenced by their previous success) may have contributed to their unsuccessful hiring of the senior-level executives. For example, participants were decisive in expressing what contributed to the failure of their unsuccessful hire, not realizing that the very qualities they attributed to the direct report's failure were the qualities that influenced their hire. One participant expressed overconfidence in his ability to select future candidates, stating, "Well, there are a couple things that I do differently now. One is, it's a level of probing that I do into the things around style and fit that are important. I dig into those in far more detail than I have in the past" (Participant 10, ll. 057).

All of these participants overestimated their ability to intuitively assess for the skills or cultural fit construct during their decision to hire the senior-level executive they described as being unsuccessful. Participant 7 had stressed collaboration:

> He also wasn't . . . interestingly, despite my efforts to determine that he would be collaborative, he made the effort to be collaborative but he did not . . . he wasn't respected and so he . . . it was a combination of things. He just really wasn't able to connect in a way that meant . . . that was totally relevant for our business and embraced by the business leaders. (ll. 181)

Although Participant 6 emphasized the participatory nature of the organizational culture, he hired an individual who was ultimately very controlling: "So he was more of a direct, top-down style and not that that's wrong, but inside a culture that's kind of bottom-up and very participatory, people all of a sudden aren't being listened to and there's much more telling going on than asking, that's a problem" (ll. 111).

Assessing candidates who have an Ivy League education can result in confirmation bias and overconfidence, as their education may have an undue influence on hiring decisions:

> So his past experience lined up with what we would want him to be doing in the future. He had an academic background that we liked, in fact I have to say again the . . . in terms of my boss talking to his board, the academic background was Ivy League and the boss liked that. (Participant 7, ll. 203)

The above examples demonstrate the participants' perceptions of the failed candidate, demonstrating that these senior executives were overconfident during the hiring of these senior-level executive direct reports and their responses suggest that they did not realize that they were overconfident during the hiring process: "That's a hollow victory for me but I am okay because I think now I've got the opportunity, having come through this, I know what I am looking for more the next time" (Participant 4, ll. 068).

Summary

Senior executives in Fortune 1000 organizations are constantly seeking new senior-level direct reports that have confirmed experience and previous contributions that are the right fit for their team and their organization. In addition, they want new senior-level leadership that is a cultural fit for their organization and a personality fit for them. Senior executives see the decision-making process and the final decision for selecting their senior-level direct reports as one of their most important responsibilities to the organization and their team.

This chapter provides answers to the two research questions and explores how senior executives use heuristics in their decision-making process for selecting senior-level direct reports (i.e., discuss one successful and one unsuccessful hiring event). Using an exploratory descriptive approach, common themes and five core categories were selected from the 13 participant interviews.

The narratives provided by senior executive participants showed their consistent use of three heuristics during their decision-making processes when selecting senior-level direct reports: availability heuristics, representative heuristics, and confirmation bias. Further, the data revealed that executives may also have been overconfident when making their hiring decisions.

Common themes included (a) the conceptualization of how senior executives use heuristics during their naturalistic and rational decision-making approach for selecting senior-level executives as their direct reports, (b) senior executives use heuristics to define and determine a senior-level executive's cultural fit, (c) senior executives use heuristics to determine personality fit and leadership style of potential senior-level direct reports, (d) senior executives combine intuitive heuristics with rational decision-making approaches to determine if a candidate's experience, previous contributions, and education are a fit for their organization, and (e) senior executives show some evidence of being overconfident in their decision-making process for selecting senior-level direct reports because of previous success. From these common themes, the decision-making processes of senior executive participants in selecting senior executive direct reports were grouped into five core categories:

1. Rational and Naturalistic Decision-Making

2. Organization Culture and Heuristics

3. Personality and Leadership Style

4. Experience, Previous Contributions, and Education

5. Senior Executives' Overconfidence Bias

The following chapter presents a discussion of the study's findings including implications for practice, limitations, and recommendations for further research.

CHAPTER FIVE: CONCLUSION AND RECOMMENDATIONS
Introduction

This study examines how senior executives use heuristics in their decision-making process to select senior-level direct reports. In qualitative interviews, each participant was asked to recall two senior-level hiring events--one that was successful and one that proved to be unsuccessful--and elaborate on how they assessed and evaluated the candidates during the hiring process. Participants' responses revealed their use of two decision-making approaches: *rational* and *naturalistic*. Further, from a foundational list of the ten most often used and well-researched heuristics that might potentially be employed by senior executives in selecting senior-level direct reports (discussed in detail in Chapter 3), three heuristics emerged from the data as used most often by the participants: *availability heuristics, representative heuristics,* and *confirmation bias.* To address the research question, five general themes that emerged from the data were grouped into five core categories: (a) rational and naturalistic decision-making; (b) organization culture and heuristics; (c) personality fit, leadership style, and heuristics; (d) experience, contributions, education, and heuristics; and (e) senior executive overconfidence bias and heuristics.

This chapter explores rational and naturalistic decision-making approaches and processes in relation to the hiring process. The chapter begins with an introduction, followed by sections on heuristics in decision-making, bias, personal observations, and further discussion. Also presented are implications for practice, theoretical implications, recommendations for further research, and a summary of findings, ending with concluding remarks.

Heuristics in Decision-Making

Decision-making research has generally focused on rational decision-making processes dating back as far as the Renaissance when scientists believed that the study of nature could help us to understand natural phenomena (Bernstein, 2004). Subsequently, researchers have studied the decision-making performance of experts on the job and in laboratories and have come to extend decision-making theory and research to include the naturalistic perspective (Adams et al., 2009). According to this perspective, people often use intuitive processes and heuristics (i.e., shortcuts) to make decisions in the real world, where the time to deliberate and incomplete information preclude the use of fully rational strategies (Cabantous, Gond, & Johnson-Cramer, 2010). Other research has also emphasized the concessions that decision makers often need to make. Simon (1969) proposed another decision-making model, arguing that because of the limited capacity of the human memory and cognitive processing limitations; decision-making capabilities are situated in a bounded rationality (i.e., limited by available information, resources, and time constraints).

Heuristics research and theory has produced mixed results. Gigerenzer and Hoffrage (2008), in their research at the Max Plank Institute for Human Development, found that applying heuristics for problem solving could lead to remarkably accurate solutions. Kahneman and Tversky's controlled experiments demonstrated that apparent cognitive-processing limitations, as well as the subject's attitudes and values, could account for a person's persistent biases. More recently, Shah and Oppenheimer (2008) posited that while heuristics are useful for reducing the effort associated with "judgment and choice," the use of heuristics could lead to errors in judgment.

This study's findings revealed that the senior executive participants rely on intuitive heuristics combined with *rational decision-making* processes when confirming a senior-level executive candidate's *experience and previous contributions.* It was also found that the senior executive participants rely on heuristics during their *naturalistic decision-making* processes when intuitively evaluating *cultural fit, personality fit,* and *leadership style* with their organization and team. Further, they rely on heuristics intuitively using a *naturalistic decision-making* process in making the *final hiring decision.* Their responses support the researcher's contention that these senior executives use heuristics throughout their decision-making process for selecting senior-level executive direct reports.

Cultural and Personality Fit

During the individual interviews, each senior executive participant was asked to describe their experiences with two hiring events—one that proved successful and one that proved unsuccessful. During the course of their narratives, all of the senior executives stressed that cultural fit was critical to the success of executives in their organizations. Yet they indicated that their organizations had no formal procedures in place to select senior-level executives for cultural and personality fit. To understand how the participants used heuristics in their decision-making process, the researcher specifically asked the participants to describe their thought process in identifying a senior-level executive as a cultural and personality fit for their organization. Participants were straightforward in their responses to this question, admitting that they could not explicitly define their organization's culture. This suggests that rather than using strict and well-defined criteria (as presumably required in a purely rational approach), they instead relied on a more naturalistic, intuitive decision-making process to make the final decision for selecting their senior-level direct reports.

All of the participants reported using a storytelling interviewing approach to assist them in making their final hiring decisions. The storytelling interview methodology seeks to collect data on specific incidents in an individual's life in an effort to better understand that person's past behavior, with the expectation that future behavior can be predicted (Creswell, 2012). This qualitative storytelling approach enabled the senior executives to make a decision about the candidate's personality fit and cultural fit with the organization during the selection process (see Shah & Oppenheimer, 2008; Simon, 1990). However, there was strong and consistent evidence that these executive relied on heuristics and their intuitions (e.g., representative and availability, confirmation bias) when assessing candidates' responses.

The senior executive participants in this study were closely aligned in how they intuitively determined whether a senior-level executive candidate was a cultural or personality fit using terms such as "collaborative," "positive," "professional," "human values," "humility," and "strong desire to work in the organization." Importantly, they argued that these attributes were more important to a senior-level executive's success than experience and previous contributions (Schneider, 1987). In this sense, then, they selectively used their intuitive judgements about candidates' characteristics rather than relying on more objective measures.

The use of confirmation bias, representative heuristics, and availability heuristics supported these senior executives' beliefs that if a senior-level direct report is missing these attributes, he or she would not adjust to the culture of the organization and would ultimately fail. Surprisingly, 12 of the 13 participants in this study, in describing an unsuccessful hiring event, suggested that the person was unsuccessful because he or she was not a cultural or personality fit for their organization. These senior executives did not realize that they had used heuristics in their decision-making process to select the senior-level direct reports that failed. This suggests that they believed that these candidates were a cultural and personality fit at the time of their selection because they used heuristics during their naturalistic decision-making process in selecting the unsuccessful senior-level direct report. This finding is similar to a study conducted by Valins and Ray (as cited in Nisbett & Wilson, 1977) illustrating that because the senior executives viewed the failed senior-level direct reports differently after a while, they used heuristics to decide how they felt about these individuals, confirming cognitively that these individuals were not a cultural or personality fit because they were not collaborative or team players.

Discussion with these senior executives reaffirmed their belief in their decision-making process for selecting senior-level direct reports, even after they described a hiring event that did not go well. This suggests that they were unaware that their reliance on heuristics may have negatively influenced their decision making. These heuristics may have led them to see a candidate as having the leadership attributes required for success in a senior-level executive role when, in fact, they did not (Adams, et al., 2009; Barnes, 1984).

This could indicate suboptimal decision-making approaches, because relying on intuitions may not give adequate weight to other important attributes required by senior-level executive candidates (Kahneman & Tversky, 1996). For example, 6 of the 13 participants indicated that they and their board members were overly impressed with candidates who were educated at an Ivy League university and they tended to offer those candidates senior-level executive positions rather than using more objective and rational indicators of the candidate's experience and previous contributions. This suggests that these senior executives used confirmation bias and representative heuristics to support their decision to hire a senior-level executive with an Ivy League education as their direct report with less concern for the candidate's experience, previous contributions, and cultural fit. Subsequently, 5 of the participants said that the Ivy League senior-level executive they hired was not successful and left their organization within one year. Again, this would indicate that reliance on intuitive factors (e.g., representative heuristics and confirmation bias) may have caused them to select a candidate that was not a cultural and personality fit for their organization (Rehak et al., 2010). This suggests that their naturalistic decision-making approaches for selecting senior-level executives were somewhat flawed.

Leadership Style

Recent research has confirmed the use of representative heuristics and confirmation bias when using a naturalistic decision-making approach to assess for leadership attributes (Keller et al., 2010; Rehak et al., 2010). The senior executive participants in this study used a naturalistic decision-making approach, and applied confirmation bias and representative heuristics to assess for leadership attributes of potential senior-level direct reports. Interestingly, leadership skills were mentioned less frequently than leadership style, cultural fit, personality fit, experience, or previous contributions. These executives described leadership style using terms such as "collaboration," "low ego," "desire," "smart," "strategic," and "executive presence." They described their assessment of leadership skills with terms such as "style," "seeing the big picture," "articulate," "pedigree," "professionalism," and "presented well." They also asked questions of the senior-level candidates to confirm the presence of these attributes prior to making their final selection decision. This information enabled them to use heuristics to make their decisions. See Chapter 4 for examples of the questions these executives used to access representative heuristics and confirmation bias.

While leadership style was a part of the evaluation process when these senior executives selected their senior-level direct reports, only 7 used confirmation bias and 9 used representative heuristics to assess the senior-level candidate's leadership style. None of the participants used availability heuristics to assess the candidates for leadership style. This would suggest that these senior executives used heuristics during their naturalistic decision-making approach to assess these senior-level executive candidates' leadership style, and further this indicates that leadership style is not as important to these senior executives as finding comfort in the candidate's cultural and personality fit construct.

Additional Themes

Five key categories emerged from the data including the conceptualization of how and when senior executives use a naturalistic or rational decision-making approach and how they apply heuristics during the application of each; cultural fit and heuristics; personality fit, leadership style, and heuristics; experience, previous contributions, education, and heuristics, and senior executives' overconfidence and heuristics.

Several additional subthemes, related to the five categories, were touched on by some of the participants during the interviews. One was the participants' use of availability heuristics to confirm a candidate's ability to be *collaborative* with senior executive peers--a key element in determining a senior-level candidate's cultural and personality fit. Conversely, all but one of the senior-executives used confirmation bias and representative heuristics in citing lack of collaboration as a key factor in an unsuccessful hire that ultimately left the organization.

Another subtheme that emerged from the data was these senior executives' general lack of concern in a candidate's ability to be a team player. Only 6 of the 13 participants included any conversation about the term *team player* during the interviewing and hiring process. Those who did used confirmation bias, representative, or availability heuristics to confirm a senior-level candidate's ability to be a team player. Only 2 of the participants cited not being a team player as the primary reason that an unsuccessful hire left the organization.

Intellect was another concept that emerged from the participants' responses. These senior executives only used confirmation bias during their naturalistic decision-making process in evaluating a candidate's *intellectual ability*. They used terms such as "super-bright," "humorous," "can't teach smart," "they can think," "can assimilate information," "draw new conclusions," and "thinking outside the box." One of the participants stated that understanding the intellect of a candidate is "really in my mind." This would indicate that these senior executives used heuristics intuitively to determine the intellectual ability of senior-level candidates.

Bias

Kahneman and Tversky (2000) found that individuals' decision-making processes are systematically flawed because of individuals' bounded rationality and the use of heuristics. Their research caused considerable debate when they argued that individuals rely on inherent preferences and intuitions, which can create predictable patterns of decision-making biases. More recently, research has confirmed that individuals' decision-making preferences follow systematic and predictable patterns because of the use of heuristics (Rehak, Adams, & Belanger, 2010).

These findings suggest that reliance on heuristics by senior executives during their rational and naturalistic decision-making processes for selecting senior-level direct reports could limit their talent selection and ultimately their return on investment because their talent pool is a representation of systematic selection of individuals with similarities. This could limit the diversity of ideas, decisions, and perspectives that a more diverse talent pool can offer.

The participants in this study were unaware of their use of heuristics or how heuristics informed their decision-making process for selecting senior-level direct reports. Further, they were not aware that their use of heuristics caused them to systematically select direct reports who represented what they perceived to be the most important characteristics of a new senior-level executive: (a) cultural fit, (b) personality fit, and (c) leadership style. These distinctions were assessed using a naturalistic decision-making approach and heuristics. In most cases, the participants in this research described their judgements about candidates related to cultural fit, personality fit, and leadership style in intuitive and heuristic-based terms rather than as part of a purely rational decision-making process. Such judgements are rather subjective and assessed from a naturalistic decision-making approach supported with heuristics.

Senior Executive Overconfidence Bias

Research has shown that overconfidence heuristics are present when individuals are unaware of the questionable assumptions that often can influence their judgment (Barnes, 1984). Senior executive participants' responses revealed that they are overconfident of their decision-making abilities in selecting successful senior-level direct reports for their organization and they apply heuristics.

Senior executives' responses in recalling an unsuccessful hiring event suggested that they explained their previous success in selecting senior-level direct reports as their most valuable asset in their hiring processes. Thus, they rarely deviated from their interviewing and decision-making process. In fact, when describing the unsuccessful senior-level hiring event, twelve of the participants attributed this to their failure to adequately scrutinize the responses of the candidates closely enough for organizational culture fit and personality fit. For example, one participant said, "I failed because I never talked to him about cultural fit." In this case, the participant indicated that he decided intuitively that the candidate was a cultural fit at the time of hire. This would suggest that this senior executive might have been overconfident and used confirmation bias, representative heuristics, and availability heuristics during his naturalistic decision-making approach for selecting the unsuccessful candidate. This supports the premise that these senior executives make their final decision to select a senior-level direct report using a subjective and intuitive decision-making approach. Using these heuristics could have decreased the amount and type of information used, resulting in a suboptimal decision (Barnes, 1984; Rehak et al., 2010; Shah & Oppenheimer, 2008). Ironically, the responses from these senior executives indicate their continued belief that following the same decision-making process for selecting future senior-level direct reports will be successful, although their processes have not necessarily resulted in the best decisions.

Personal Observations

During my 20 years of executive experience with two Fortune 1000 organizations, I observed that the hiring practices at both organizations followed distinct patterns, but that hiring for a cultural fit was especially paramount for one of the organizations. I observed in both organizations that when senior executives were making the final decision to select a senior-level direct report, they abandoned the organization's rational assessments and always made the final decision naturalistically using heuristics, although I could not explain their decision-making approach at the time.

Because of my close relationship to this process, my ability to intuitively assess for perceived talent using heuristics improved to the point that I led many of the interviewing and selection processes at both organizations. Subsequently, I found that the successful candidates in both organizations were evaluated during the interview process as having the required experience and previous contributions using a rational decision-making approach and heuristics; they were assessed for personality fit and cultural fit intuitively using heuristics as part of a naturalistic decision-making approach. Conversely, most of the new hires that were ultimately unsuccessful were labeled as "not a cultural fit," although they were hired because they were previously determined to be a cultural fit during the selection process. During these assessments, I would find myself occasionally uncomfortable because the final selection decision was only supported by intuition and subjectivity within both organizations whose senior executive teams shared exclusive similarities.

Because of these observations during my executive career, my interest regarding senior executive decision-making for hiring senior-level direct reports emerged. Thus, I focused my research on learning how senior executives describe their decision-making process for selecting senior-level direct reports in an effort to better understand why they generally selected individuals who were similar in many respects. I did not believe that senior executives were cognizant of their systematic selection of individuals with personal similarities intuitively, and I did not believe that they were cognitively aware of any potentially biased behavior associated with their decision-making process when selecting subordinates. More importantly, with the changing American demographics, I wanted to learn why there were fewer women and minority senior-level executives in Fortune 1000 organizations (Embrick, 2011).

Discussion

This study's findings revealed that, although 77% of the participants were from different organizations, they all assessed potential new hires for cultural fit and personality fit using heuristics intuitively in attempting to identify and confirm the same characteristics in senior-level candidates that matched those of previously hired candidates. Participants believe they can adequately evaluate candidates for these characteristics in a one-hour interview, over dinner, or on the golf course, and they believe that their final hiring decision is rational.

It is no wonder that the use of a naturalistic decision-making approach has the potential to lead to consistently similar decisions. Admittedly, many of their final hiring decisions proved ultimately successful, however reliance on heuristics when selecting senior-level direct reports likely also caused systematic errors in their decision-making process. For example, these senior executives continued to follow the same decision-making processes (i.e., relying on heuristics) for selecting senior-level direct reports whom they believed to be a cultural fit for their organization when, in fact, their decision-making process had previously proven to be flawed.

Nisbett and Wilson's (1977) review of the literature found that humans are introspectively certain about their cognitive abilities when the perceived evidence is (a) minimal and (b) available or cognitively salient; (c) where a cultural rule can predict the outcome; and (d) where the causes are represented by previous outcomes (p. 255). Several of the participants used heuristics that suggest that they hire people who are similar to themselves. This was evident in their use of terms such as "it's a family," "he's a golfer," "same nationality," "packaging," and even "just like me." The use of heuristics in this context supports previous research suggesting that senior-executives systematically hire individuals who match themselves (Embrick, 2011). Tversky and Kahneman (1974) proposed that individuals judge the probability of an event occurrence based on the availability of the frequency and probability of the event at the time of the decision being made. This research suggests that senior executives may use heuristics because they reduce the effort associated with processing information during decision-making. Given the need to choose among several candidates with diverse skills and characteristics, then, executives may inadvertently default to relying on similarity to make their judgements, as relying on known sources of information (Rehak, et al., 2010; Shah & Oppenheimer, 2008) may simplify the decision-making process.

An unexpected outcome that surfaced in this study was the finding that none of the participants considered whether the individuals they hired were familiar with elements in their organization's environment through past experiences, to include childhood. New senior-level executives who proved successful may well have adjusted to the culture of the organization after employment and may not have initially been a "cultural fit" as perceived during the assessment process (Bandura, 2002). As previously noted, in response to the interview question to describe a hiring event that ultimately proved unsuccessful, 12 of the participants attributed the new senior-level executive's failure to not being a cultural fit for the organization, although they had previously evaluated and confirmed the newly hired senior-level executive as a cultural fit. This is further confirmation that these participants' cognitive understanding of their decision-making process is limited and subject to systematic flaws because of their use of heuristics in selecting senior-level direct reports (Nesbett & Wilson, 1977).

Implications for Practice

Although the senior executive participants believed they used a rational decision-making approach in evaluating potential senior-level direct reports for hire, the findings of this study reveal that they ultimately relied on a naturalistic or intuitive process. Senior executives should consider relevant criteria to review the pros and cons of their naturalistic, or intuitive decision-making process in selecting a candidate based on perceived cultural fit, personality fit, or leadership style, to ensure that they have objectively considered all the evidence and that nothing was overlooked (Adams et al., 2009). They would do well to combine both rationalistic and naturalistic approaches. This could include adopting a multifaceted approach to include obtaining input from an objective outside source regarding their decision-making process prior to final selection in addition to their intuitive judgements. This is contrary to the norm in executive hiring, where it is the candidate who is generally assessed by an outside agency. These steps could assist senior executives in identifying any heuristics they may have used during the decision-making process, thereby improving the overall quality and results of their decision in selecting senior-level direct reports.

Research has shown that while the use of heuristics is relevant to both naturalistic and rational decision-making approaches, they are most active intuitively during the naturalistic decision-making process and can lead to systematically biased decisions (Adams et al., 2009; Barnes, 1984; Nesbett & Wilson, 1977; Shah & Oppenheimer, 2008; Tversky & Kahneman, 1974). Thus, senior executives should be particularly cautious when assessing for cultural fit, personality fit, or leadership style during their decision-making process for selecting senior-level direct reports to ensure that they are not systematically making selections based on the most available or representative knowledge that is cognitively present during the selection process. This will allow for consideration of a broader group of candidates. The findings that the use of heuristics can lead to systematically biased decisions should be reason enough to consider revising the interviewing and assessment approach for selecting senior-level direct reports.

Implications for Theory

This study provided the opportunity to support the work of many scholars who researched and studied decision-making theory and heuristics dating back more than 50 years (Adams et al., 2009; Brehmer, et al., 1986; Gigerenzer, 2008; Kahneman & Tversky, 2000; Shah & Oppenheimer, 2008; Simon, 1947). The research and theories of these scholars and many others suggest that humans use heuristics in their daily lives. The use of heuristics can provide a fast, effective, and efficient decision-making process that often delivers satisfactory responses. However, the reliance on heuristics can lead to systematically biased decisions (Rehak et al., 2010). Similarly, this study found that while the participants' use of heuristics generally delivers satisfactory results when selecting senior-level direct reports, it also demonstrated that their decision-making process is occasionally flawed because of the use of heuristics. Using heuristics, one research participant stated, "you need calming personalities, not, you know, 'Hi, I'm a Harvard MBA.'"

Current theories of how humans use heuristics in their decision-making process were confirmed during this study. However, the use of heuristics in naturalistic and rational decision-making for selecting senior-level direct reports offered a departure point for this study's data collection and analysis. To date, no documented qualitative study has identified the cognitive components involved in how senior executives use heuristics during their rational or naturalistic decision-making process, and no documented qualitative study has identified the heuristics used by senior executives in the hiring process. Thus, this study contributes to the general literature on the decision-making process as well as the use of heuristics, and specifically, for senior executives who are assessing senior-level direct reports for a final hiring decision.

Recommendations for Further Research

Because of the limited number of senior executive participants for this research project, it is recommended that a more comprehensive qualitative study be conducted to better understand how the use of heuristics during a rational and naturalistic decision-making approach can hinder or improve the decision-making process of senior executives for selecting senior-level direct reports. More specifically, it is recommended that a more extensive qualitative study be completed to understand why senior executives use a naturalistic decision-making approach and heuristics exclusively to assess potential senior-level direct reports for cultural and personality fit before they make a final hiring decision. A larger participant pool might reveal how reliance on certain heuristics might be minimized, enabling a more diverse group of candidates to be considered for senior executive positions in Fortune 1000 organizations (see Embrick, 2011). Further, a similar study might be replicated with senior executives from different industries other than this study's population of Fortune 1000 retail and hotel organizations.

This study used a foundation of 10 most commonly applied and well-researched heuristics, resulting in 3 used primarily by the senior executive participants in this study.

A more comprehensive study might expand the number of heuristics used for initial consideration during the analysis of the results to associate more of the participants' responses to specific heuristics for a more complete analysis of the responses to the interview questions. The addition of more heuristics for analysis would help to ensure that the primary heuristics used by senior executives during their rational and naturalistic decision-making approach for selecting senior-level direct reports, as identified by the researcher in this study, could be replicated in other qualitative and quantitative studies.

Another categorical theme that emerged from the research on how senior executives use heuristics during their decision-making process for selecting senior-level direct reports was the participants' lack of awareness that the successful candidates they hired may have adjusted to the culture and environment of their organization because of familiarity with a corporate culture (Bandura, 2002). While all the study participants indicated that a cultural fit was the most important consideration for hiring a senior-level direct report, there was no recognized recommendation to find a way to perhaps enable the organizational culture to be more conducive to hiring otherwise qualified candidates. Because these participants did not offer any evidence contrary to their core belief that all of their potential senior-level direct reports must be a cultural fit, it is recommended that further qualitative and quantitative research methods explore this dilemma.

Additionally, it is recommended that senior executives seek advice on their decision-making process for selecting senior-level direct reports to better understand how their decision-making approaches can be influenced by the use of heuristics. Understanding their own decision-making process and how the use of heuristics can cause systematically biased decisions might allow senior executives to select senior-level candidates from a broader and more diverse population, thereby positioning their organization to be more competitive in a global economy of rapidly changing demographics (see Embrick, 2011). Nisbett and Wilson (1977) argued that because individuals feel that they have direct access to their own cognitive process they might evaluate a person in a certain way, but in fact, people have little direct access to their "own cognitive processes" (p. 255). This would suggest that individuals should be more challenging of their own decision-making process to ensure that they minimize the use of heuristics. It would also be interesting to explore why senior executives engage virtually no rational decision-making in assessing senior-level executive candidates who have an Ivy League education. The results of this research found that 38% of the participants in this study indicated that they had hired an Ivy League-educated senior-level direct report who ultimately proved to be an unsuccessful hire.

The researcher's finding that the study participants were overconfident in their decision-making process for selecting senior-level direct reports is important because it suggests that the participants did not realize that their decision-making process could be flawed. Although some of the senior executives made adjustments to their decision-making process after they selected a senior-level candidate that failed, the adjustments were focused on reassuring themselves that future candidates met their criteria for a cultural and personality fit. Thus, they determined to ask more questions to confirm intuitively that the candidates were a cultural fit using a naturalistic decision-making process and heuristics. Nisbett and Wilson (1977) found that individuals are cognitively inclined to be overconfident and believe in their own "predictions and subjective control" because not believing in their ability to make rational decisions is too frightening (p. 257). Further research is recommended to determine if overconfidence and self-reinforcement extends to disciplines and organizations other than those described in this study.

Previous research has suggested that senior executives systematically hire individuals who match themselves (Embrick, 2011). Although several of the participants used terms to suggest that this is true, it is important to note that not all the participants responded in this context, and that the organizations selected for this research were predominately traditional retail organizations historically led by Caucasian males. Further research and analysis is warranted to determine how the use of heuristics during senior executives' rational and naturalistic decision-making process for selecting senior-level direct reports has influenced diversity in the senior executive ranks in Fortune 1000 organizations. Regardless of their responses, it is this researcher's opinion that the participants in this study were not cognizant of any bias in their decision-making process for selecting senior-level direct reports. However, based on the responses from these participants, this study showed that their final decision for selecting a senior-level direct report was intuitive and influenced by heuristics.

Summary of Findings

Through a qualitative thematic approach, 13 senior executives were interviewed about their perceptions of their decision-making process in selecting senior-level direct reports. Their responses revealed the heuristics most commonly used by these senior executives and how these heuristics are connected to both rational and naturalistic decision-making.

Participants' responses were grouped into general themes to include the following findings:

- Senior executives use both a *rational* and *naturalistic decision-making approach* for selecting senior-level direct reports.

- Senior executives make use of various heuristics in the decision-making process, primarily *representative heuristics, availability heuristics,* and *confirmation bias.*

- Senior executives believe that a cultural fit is most critical to the success of new executives in their organizations, but they could not explicitly define their organization's culture. Thus, they use a *naturalistic*, or intuitive decision-making approach and they apply heuristics to determine the *cultural fit* of a potential new senior-level report.

- Senior executives follow a *naturalistic* decision-making approach and apply heuristics when evaluating the *personality fit* and *leadership style* of potential senior-level direct reports.

- Senior executives follow a *rational* decision-making approach and apply heuristics when evaluating the *experience, previous contributions,* and *education* of potential senior-level direct reports.

- Senior executives are *overconfident* of their decision-making abilities for selecting successful senior-level direct reports for their organization. The participants conceptualized their decision-making process as being situated in a rational domain when, in fact, their final hiring decision is situated in a naturalistic, intuitive decision-making domain guided by the use of heuristics.

Conclusion

This research supports the contention that heuristics are present in the decision-making process of individuals. While heuristics are generally used to support satisfactory decision-making, their use can lead to systematically biased judgment (Barnes, 1984; Gigerenzer, 2008; Shah & Oppenheimer, 2008). Specific to this study, understanding the decision-making process used by senior executives in selecting senior-level direct reports can assist in identifying how they conceptualize the components of, and identify the heuristics that inform their decision-making. Further, determining the importance that senior executives place on each component of their decision-making process may assist in improving their decision-making in selecting senior-level direct reports, ultimately increasing the talent pool to include broader and more diverse population, and thereby positioning their organization to be more competitive in a global economy of rapidly changing demographics.

When all is said and done, humans will continue to use heuristics to make everyday decisions as well as complex, critical decisions about their lives, families, and subordinates. Understanding how we use heuristics and how the use of heuristics can influence the outcome of our decisions can assist us in making better, more informed decisions and serve to reduce poor judgment and bias in the decisions that we make.

References

Adams, B. D., Rehak, L., Brown, A., & Hall, C.T. (2009). *Human decision-making biases.* Report Produced for Defense Research and Development Canada, HumanSystems Incorporated, Guelph, Ontario, Canada.

Abebe, M. A., Angriawan, A., & Liu, Y. (2010). CEO power and organizational turnaround in declining firms: Does environment play a role? *Journal of Leadership & Organizational Studies, 18(2),* 260-271.

Alexander, P. A. (2004). The development of expertise: The journey from acclimation to proficiency. *Educational Researcher, 32*, 10-14.

Allport, G. W. (1954). *The nature of prejudice.* Oxford, England: Addison-Wesley.

Arendt, L. A., Priem, R. L., & Ndofor, H. A. (2005). A CEO-Adviser model of strategic decision making. *Journal of Management, 31(5),* 680-690.

Aristotle. (2007). Rhetoric. (W. R. Roberts, Trans.). Retrieved August 18, 2012, from ebooks@Adelaide at http://ebooks.adelaide.edu.au/a/aristotle/a8rh/

Bacchus, N. J. (2004). The underrepresentation of black male executives and CEOs in Fortune 500 corporations (doctoral dissertation, Capella University, 2004). *ProQuest Information and Learning Company,* UMi 3162633.

Baker, D. A. (2010). Enhancing group decision making: An exercise to reduce shared information bias. *Journal of Management Education, 34*(2), 249-279.

Bandura, A. (2002). Social cognitive theory in cultural context. *Applied Psychology: An International Review 51* (2) 269-290.

Banks, C. A. M. (1995). Gender and race as factors in educational leadership and administration. In J. A. Banks & C.A.M. Banks (Eds.), *Handbook of research on multicultural education* (2nd ed., pp. 65-80). New York, NY: Macmillan.

Barkan, R., & Busemeyer, J. R. (2003). Modeling dynamic inconsistency with a changing reference point. *Journal of Behavioral Decision Making, 16*, 235-255.

Barnes, J. (1984). Cognitive biases and their impact on strategic planning. *Strategic Management Journal*, 5, 129-137.

Baron, J. N., & Pfeffer, J. (1994). The social psychology of organizations and inequality. *Social Psychology Quarterly, 57*, 190-209.

Baumeister, R. F. (1998). The self. In D. T. Gilbert, S. T. Fiske & G. Lindzey (Eds.), *The handbook of social psychology, vols. 1 & 2* (4th ed., pp. 680-740). New York, NY: McGraw-Hill.

Bazerman, M. H. (2001). The study of real decision making. *Journal of Behavioral Decision Making, 14,* 353-355.

Bean, M. G., Slaten, D.G., Horton, S. W., Murphy, M. C., Todd, R. A., & Richeson, J. A. (in press). Prejudice concerns and race-based attentional bias: New evidence from eyetracking. *Social Psychological and Personality Science*.

Bechtel, W., & Abrahamsen, A. (1991). *Connectionism and the mind: An introduction to parallel processing in networks.* Oxford, England: Basil Blackwell.

Bell, C. S. (1998). Organizational Influences on women's experience in the superintendency. *Peabody Journal of Education, 65*(4), 31-59.

Bensimon, E. M., Neumann, A., & Birnbaum, R. (1989). *Making sense of administrative leadership*: The "L" word in higher education, ASHE-ERIC Higher Education Report. Washington, DC: School of Education, George Washington University.

Bernstein, J. (2004). *Against the gods*: *The remarkable story of risk.* New York, NY: John

Wiley & Sons.

Biederman, I. (1987). Recognition-by-components: A theory of human image understanding. *Psychological Review, 94*, 115-147.

Boone, C., Van Olffen, W., Witteloostuijn, A. V., & De Brabander (2004). The genesis of top management team diversity: Selective turnover among top management teams in Dutch newspaper publishing. *Academy of Management Journal, 47(5)*, 633-656.

Botvinick, M., Kool, W., McGuire, J. T., & Rosen, Z. B. (2010). Decision making and the avoidance of cognitive demand. *Journal of Experimental Psychology, 139(4)*, 665-682.

Boumans, M. (2008). Battle in the planning office: Field experts versus normative statisticians. *Social Epistemology, 22*, 389-404.

Boumans, M. (2011). The two-model problem in rational decision making. *Rationality and Society, 23(3)*, 371-400.

Braddock, J., & McPartland, J. (1986). Applicant race and job placement decisions: A national survey experiment. *International Journal of Sociology and Social Policy 6*(1), 3-24.

Brehmer, B., Jungerman, H., Lourens, P., & Sevon, G. (1986). *New directions in research on decision making.* Amsterdam, NY: North-Holland.

Brewer, M. B. (1988). A dual process model of impression formation. In T. K. Srull & R.S. Wyer (Eds.), *Advances in social cognition* (vol. 1, pp. 1-36). Hillsdale, NJ: Lawrence Erlbaum.

Brousseau, K.N., Driver, M. J., Hourihan, G., & Larsson, R. (2006). The seasoned executive's decision-making style. *Harvard Business Review, 84*(2), 110-121.

Busenitz, L. W., & Barney, J. B. (1997). Biases and heuristics in strategic decision making: Differences between entrepreneurs and managers in large organizations. *Journal of Business Venturing, 12*(1), 9-30.

Cabantous, L., Gond, P.J., & Johnson-Cramer, M. (2010). Decision theory as practice: Crafting rationality in organizations. *Organizational Studies, 31*(11), 1531-1566.

Cable, D. M., & Judge, T. A. (1997). Interviewers' perception of person-organizational fit and organizational selection decisions. *Journal of Applied Psychology, 82*(4), 546-561.

Cantor, D. W., & Bernay, T. (1992). *Women in power: The secret of leadership.* New York, NY: Houghton Mifflin

Carmeli, A., Gelbard, R., & Gefen, D. (2010). The importance of innovation leadership in cultivating strategic fit and enhancing firm performance. *The Leadership Quarterly, 21*, 339-349.

Carmeli, A., Schaubroeck, J., & Tishler, A. (2011). How CEO empowering leadership shapes top management teams processes: Implications for firm performance. *The Leadership Quarterly, 21,* 339-349.

Carmeli, A., Tishler, A., & Edmondson, A. C. (2012). CEO relational leadership and strategic decision quality in top management teams: The role of team trust and learning from failure. *Strategic Organization, 10*(1), 31-54.

Castilla, E. J. (2008). Gender, race, and meritocracy in organizational careers. *American Journal of Sociology, 113*, 1379-1526.

Chi, M. T. H., Glaser, R., & Farr, M. J. (1988). *The nature of expertise.* Hillsdale, NJ: Lawrence Erlbaum Associates.

Colman, L. (2006). *Why managers and companies take risks*. Parkville, Victoria: The University of Melbourne.

Cone, J., & Foster, S. (2006). *Dissertations and theses from start to finish* (2nd ed.). Washington, DC: American Psychological Association.

Correll, J., Urland, G. R., & Ito, T. A. (2006). Event-related potentials and the decision to shoot: The role of treat perception and cognitive control. *Journal of Experimental Social Psychology, 42*, 120-128.

Creswell, J. (2003). *Research design: Qualitative, quantitative, and mixed methods*. Thousands Oaks, CA: Sage.

Creswell, J. (2007). *Educational research: Planning, conducting, and evaluating quantitative and qualitative research* (3rd ed.). Upper Saddle River, NJ: Pearson.

Creswell, J. (2012). *Education research: Planning, conducting, and evaluating quantitative and qualitative research* (4th ed.). Upper Saddle River, NJ: Pearson.

Croskerry, P. (2000). The cognitive imperative: Thinking about how we think. *Academic Emergency Medicine, 7*, 1223-1231.

Csikszentmihalyi, M., & Figurski, T. J. (1982). Self-awareness and aversive experience in everyday life. *Journal of Personality, 50,* 16-28.

Cyert, R., & March, J. (1963). *A behavioral theory of the firm.* Englewood Cliffs, NJ: Prentice Hall.

Daft, R. L., Sormunen, J., & Parks, D. (1988). Chief executive scanning, environmental characteristics, and company performance: An empirical study. *Strategic Management Journal*, 9, 123-139.

Da Silva, A., Hutcheson, J., & Wahl, G. D. (2010). Organizational strategy and employee outcomes: A person-organization fit perspective. *The Journal of Psychology, 144*(2), 145-161.

Dawes, R. M., Faust, D., & Meehl, P. E. (1989). Clinical versus actuarial. *Judgment Science, 243*, 1668-1674.

DeGroot, A. D. (1965). *Thought and choice in chess.* The Hague, Netherlands: Mouton.

Dencker, J. C. (2008). Corporate restructuring and sex differences in managerial promotion. *American Sociological Review, 73,* 455-476.

Eagly, A., & Carli, L. (2007). Women and the labyrinth of leadership. *Harvard Business Review, 85(9),* 63-71.

Eberhardt, J. L., Goff, P, A., Purdie, V. J., & Davis, P. G. (2004). Seeing black: Race, crime and visual processing. *Journal of Personality and Social Psychology, 87*, 876-893.

Embrick, D. G. (2011). The diversity ideology in the business world: A new oppression for a new age. *Critical Sociology. 37(5)*, 541-556.

Enz, C. A. (1988). The role of value congruity in intraorganizational power. *Administrative Science Quarterly, 33*, 284-304.

Ericsson, K., Ander, P., & Cokely, E. (2007). The making of an expert. *Harvard Business Review, 85*(7/8), 114-121.

Fernandez, J. P. (1999). *Race, gender, and rhetoric: The true state of race and gender relations in corporate America.* New York, NY: McGraw-Hill.

Fetterman, D. (2010). *Ethnography: Step-by-step applied research methods* (3rd ed.). Thousands Oaks, CA: Sage Publications.

Finkelstein, S. (1992). Power in top management teams: Dimensions, measurement, and validation. *Academy of Management Journal, 35*, 505-538.

Finn, W. (2007). How to survive a scandal. *Director, 60*(12), 33.

Fiske, S., & Taylor, S. (1991). *Social cognition.* New York, NY: McGraw-Hill.

Fiske, S. T., & Neuberg, S. L. (1990). A continuum model of impression formation, from category-based to individuating processes: Influences of information and motivation on attention and interpretation. In M. P. Zanna (Ed.), *Advances in experimental social psychology* (Vol. 23, pp. 1-74). San Diego, CA: Academic Press.

Flaming, S. C. (2007). Leadership of risk decision making in a complex technology organization: The deliberative decision making model. (Capella University). *ProQuest Dissertations & Theses* (PQDT 3283782).

Forlani, D. (2002). Risk and rationality: The influence of decision domain and perceived outcome control on managers' high-risk decisions. *Journal of Behavioral Decision Making, 15*, 125-140.

Fraenkel, J., & Wallen, N. (2006). *How to design and evaluate research in education* (6th ed.). New York, NY: McGraw Hill.

Frankl, M. (2010). Heuristics-based decision-making in small and medium Canadian business (Doctoral dissertation, University of Victoria Canada, 2010). *ProQuest Dissertations & Theses (PQDT) NR74108.*

Gay, L. (1996). *Educational research: Competencies for analysis and application.* Upper Saddle River, NJ: Merrill.

Giberson, R. T., Resick, C. J., Dickson, M. W., Mitchelson, J. K., Randall, K. R., & Clark, M. A. (2009). Leadership and organizational culture: Linking CEO characteristics to cultural values. *Journal of Business Psychology, 24,* 123-147.

Gigerenzer, G. (2000). *Adaptive thinking: Rationality in the real world.* Oxford, England: Oxford University Press.

Gigerenzer, G. (2008). Why heuristics work. *Perspectives on Psychological Science, 3,* 20-29.

Gigerenzer, G., & Hoffrage, U. (2008). Fast and frugal heuristics are plausible model of cognition: Reply of Dougherty, Franco-Watkins, and Thompson (2008). *Psychological Review, 115*(1), 230-239.

Gorman, E. H. (2005). Gender stereotypes, same-gender preferences, and organizational variation in the hiring of women: Evidence from law firms. *American Sociological Review, 70,* 702-728.

Hambrick, D. C. (2007). Upper echelons theory: An update. *Academy of Management Review, 32(2),* 334-343

Hambrick, D. C., & Mason, P. A. (1984). Upper echelons: The organization as a reflection of its top managers. *Academy of Management Review, 9,* 193-206.

Hastie, R. (1981). Schematic principles in human memory. In E. Higgins, C. Herman, & M. Zanna (Eds.), *Social cognition: The Ontario Symposium* (Vol. 1, pp. 39-88). Hillsdale, NJ: Lawrence Erlbaum.

Hicks, J.L., Marsh, R. L., & Ritschel, L. (2001). The role of recollection and partial information in source monitoring. *Journal of Experimental Psychology: Learning, Memory, and Cognition, 28(3)*), 503-508. Doi: 1037/0278-7393.28.3.503.

Hilbert, M. (2011). Toward a synthesis of cognitive biases: How noisy information processing can bias human decision making. *American Psychological Association,*

138(2), 211-237.

Hinkle, C. L., & Kuehn, A. A. (1966). Heuristic models: Mapping the maze for management. *California Management Review, 10*(1), 59-60.

Hoffman, R. R., & Militello, L. G. (2008). *Perspectives on cognitive task analysis: Historical origins and modern communities of practice.* Boca Raton, FL: CRC Press/Taylor & Francis.

Hogarth, R. M. (1980). *Judgment and choice: The psychology of decisions.* New York, NY: Wiley.

Hollenbeck, G. P. (2002). Room at the top for wise choices. *In Focus, 22.*

Huey, B. M., & Wickens, C. D. (1993). *Workload transition: Implications for individuals and team performance.* Washington, DC: National Academy Press.

Iberra, H. (1992). Homophily and differential returns: Sex differences in network structure and access in an advertising firm. *Administrative Science Quarterly, 37*, 422-447.

Kahneman, D., Slovic, P., & Tversky, A. (1982). *Judgment under uncertainty: Heuristics and biases.* Cambridge, UK: Cambridge University Press.

Kahneman, D., & Tversky, A. (Eds.). (1996). On the reality of cognitive illusions. *Psychological Review. 103*(3), 582-591.

Kahneman, D., & Tversky, A. (Eds.). (2000). *Choices, values, and frames.* Cambridge, NY: University Press.

Kalantari, B. (2010). Herbert A. Simon on making decisions: Enduring insights and bounded rationality. *Journal of Management History, 16(4),* 509-520.

Keller, N., Cokely, E. T., Katsikopoulos, K. V., & Wegwarth, O. (2010). Naturalistic heuristics for decision making. *Journal of Cognitive Engineering and Decision Making, 4*(3), 256-274.

Kerr, N. L., Kramer, G. P., & MacCoun, R. J. (1996). Bias in judgment: Comparing individuals and groups. *Psychological Review, 103*(4), 687-719.

Kerr, N. L., & Tindale, R. S. (2004). Group performance and decision making. *Annual Review of Psychology, 55*, 623-655.

Kleider, H. M., Pezdek, K., Goldinger, S. D., & Kirk, A. (2008). Schema-driven source misattribution errors: Remembering the expected from a witnessed event. *Applied Cognitive Psychology, 22(1)*, 1-20.

Kirschenman, J., & Neckerman, K. (1991). "We'd love to hire them but...": The meaning of race for employers. In C. Jencks & P. Peterson (Eds.), *The urban underclass* (pp. 203-234). Washington, DC: Brookings Institution.

Kuhn, T. (1996). *The structure of scientific revolutions* (3rd ed). Chicago, IL: University of Chicago Press.

Lipshitz, R., Klein, G., Orasanu, J., & Salas, E. (2001). Taking stock of naturalistic decision making. *Journal of Behavioral Decision Making, 14*, 331-352.

Lopes, L. L. (1997). Between hope and fear: The psychology of risk. In W. M. Goldstein & R. M. Hogarth (Eds.), *Research on judgment and decision making: Currents, connections and controversies.* Cambridge, England: Cambridge University Press.

Lord, R. G., & Maher, K. J. (1991). *Leadership and information processing: Linking perception and performance.* Boston, MA: Unwin Hyman.

Lorge, I., Fox, D., Davitz, & Brenner, M. A. (1958). A survey of studies contrasting the

quality of group performance and individual performance, 1920-1957.
Psychological Bulletin, 55, 337-372.

Lounsbury, M. (2008). Institutional rationality and practice variation: New directions in the institutional analysis of practice. *Accounting, Organizations, and Society, 33*(4), 349-362.

Mamaghani, F. (2006). Impact of information technology on the workforce of the future: An analysis. *International Journal of Management, 23*(4), 845-850.

March, J., & Olsen, J. P. (1976). *Ambiguity and choice in organizations.* Bergen, Norway: Universitesforlaget.

March, J. G., & Simon, H. A. (1958). *Organizations.* New York, NY: Wiley.

Marsden, P. V. (1987). Core discussion networks of Americans. *American Sociological Review, 52*, 122-131.

Mcllwee, J., & Robinson, G. (1992). *Women in engineering: Gender, power, and workplace culture.* Albany: State University of New York Press.

Merriam-Webster (2012). Bias. Retrieved November 23, 2012 from http://www.merriam-webster.com/dictionary/bias

Merriam-Webster (2012). Heuristics. Retrieved December 4, 2012 from http://www.merriam-webster.com/dictionary/heuristics

Mitzberg, H. (1973). Strategy making in three modes. *California Management Review, 16*(2), 44-53.

Moustakas, C. (1994). *Phenomenological research methods.* Thousands Oaks, CA: Sage.

Neill, J. (2007). Qualitative versus quantitative research: Key points in a classic debate. *Research methods*. Retrieved Marched 3, 2012 from http://wilderdom.com/research/QualitativeVersusQuantitativeResearch.html#Features

Neuman, W. (2006). *Social research methods: Quantitative and qualitative approaches* (6th ed.). Boston, MA: Allyn & Bacon.

Newell, A., & Simon, H. A. (1972). *Human problem solving.* Englewood Cliffs, NJ: Prentice-Hall.

Nisbett, R. E., & Wilson, T. D. (1977). Telling more than we can know: Verbal reports on mental processes. *Psychological Review, 84*(3), 231-259.

Offermann, L. R., & Phan, L. U. (2002). *Culturally intelligent leadership for a diverse world.* In R. E. Riggio, S. E. Murphy, & F. J. Pirozzolo (Eds.), *Multiple intelligences and leadership* (pp. 187-214). Mahwah, NJ: Lawrence Erlbaum Associates.

Palmarini, M. (1994). *Inevitable illusions: How mistakes of reason rule our minds.* New York, NY: John Wiley & Sons.

Petersen, T., & Saporta, I. (2004). The opportunity structure for discrimination. *American Journal of Sociology, 109*, 852-901.

Pfeffer, J., & Salancik, R. G. (1978). *The external control of organizations: A resource dependent perspective.* New York, NY: Harper & Row.

Plous, S. (1993). *The psychology of judgment and decision making.* New York, NY: McGraw-Hill.

Popham, W. (2005). *Assessment for educational leaders.* Boston, MA: Pearson.

Priem, R. L., & Harrison, D. A. (1994). Exploring strategic judgment: Methods for testing the assumptions of prescriptive contingency theories. *Strategic Management Journal, 15*, 311-324.

Qing, C., Maruping, L. M., & Takeuchi, R. (2006). Disentangling the effects of CEO turnover and succession on organizational capabilities: A social network perspective. *Organization Science, 17*(5), 563-576.

Rehak, L. A., Adams, B., & Belanger, M. (2010). Mapping biases to the components of rationalistic and naturalistic decision making. *Proceedings of the Human Factors and Ergonomics Society annual meeting*, 54, 324-328.

Reskin, B. F., & Bielby, D. D. (2005). A sociological perspective on gender and career outcomes. *Journal of Economic Perspectives, 19*, 72-86.

Resnick, M. L. (2009). Overcoming bias in the deliberations of distributed teams. *Proceedings of the Human Factors and Ergonomics Society Annual Meeting, 53,* 444-448.

Royster, D. A. (2003). *Race and the invisible hand: How White networks exclude Black men from blue-collar jobs*. Los Angeles: University of California Press.

Ruef, M., Aldrich, H. E., & Carter, N. M. (2003). The structure of founding teams: Homophily, strong ties, and isolation among U.S. entrepreneurs. *American Sociological Review, 68*, 195-222.

Saldana, J. (2009). The coding manual for qualitative researchers. Thousand Oaks, CA: Sage Publications Ltd.

Schein, E. H. (2004). *Organizational culture and leadership* (3rd ed.). San Francisco, CA: Jossey-Bass.

Schneider, B. (1983a). Interactional psychology and organizational behavior. In L. L. Cummings & B. M. Staw (Eds.), *Research in organization behavior* (pp. 1-31). Greenwich, CT: JAI Press.

Schneider, B. (1983b). An interactionist perspective on organizational effectiveness. In K. S. Cameron & D. S. Whetten (Eds.), *Organizational effectiveness: A comparison of multiple models* (pp. 27-54). New York, NY: Academic Press.

Schneider, B. (1987). The people make the place. *Personnel Psychology*, 40, 437-453.

Schwenk, C. R. (1984). Cognitive simplification processes in strategic decision making. *Strategic Management Journal, 5*, 111-128.

Schwenk, C. R. (1988). The cognitive perspective on strategic decision making. *Journal of Management Studies, 25*, 1.

Schwenk, C. R. (1995). Strategic decision making. *Journal of Management, 21*(3), 471-494.

Sebestik, J. (2011). Bolzano's logic. *The Stanford encyclopedia of philosophy.* (E. N. Zalta, Ed.). Retrieved from http://plato.stanford.edu/archives/win2011/entries/bolzano-logic/

Shah, A. K., & Oppenheimer, D. M. (2008). Heuristics made easy: An effort-reduction framework. *Psychological Bulletin, 134*, 207-222.

Simon, H. (1969). *The science of the artificial* (3rd ed.). Cambridge, MA: MIT Press.

Simon, H. (1990). Invariants of human behavior. *Annual Review of Psychology, 41*, 1-19.

Simon, H. (1996). *The sciences of the artificial* (3rd ed). Cambridge, MA: The MIT Press.

Simon, H. A. (1947). *Administrative behavior*. New York, NY: Free Press.

Simon, H. A. (1997). *Models of bounded rationality: Empirically grounded economic reasons* (vol. 3). Cambridge, MA: MIT Press.

Spaniol, J., & Bayen, U. J. (2001). When is schematic knowledge used in source monitoring? *Journal of Experimental Psychology: Learning, Memory, and Cognition, 28(4)*, 631-651.

Stangor, C., Lynch, L., Duan, C., & Glass, B. (1992). Categorization of individuals on the basis of multiple social features. *Journal of Personality and Social Psychology, 62*, 207-218.

Thomas, A. S., & Simerly, R. L. (1994). The chief executive officer and corporate social performance: An interdisciplinary examination. *Journal of Business Ethics, 13*(12), 959-968.

Trice, H., & Beyer, J. M. (1993). *The cultures of work organizations*. Englewood Cliffs, NJ: Prentice Hall.

Turk, W. (2007). Manager or leader? *Defense AT & L, 36*(4), 20-22

Tversky, A., & Kahneman, D. (1974). Judgment under uncertainty: Heuristics and biases. *Science,* 185, 1124-1131.

Tversky, A., & Kahneman, D. (2000). Judgment under uncertainty: Heuristics and biases. In T. Conolly, H. R. Arkes, & K. R. Hammond (Eds.), *Judgment and decision making* (2nd ed., pp. 35-52). New York, NY: Cambridge University.

U.S. Department of Labor. (2010, February). *Job patterns for minorities and women in private industry (EEO-1)*. Retrieved on February 29, 2012 from http://ww1.eeoc.gov/eeoc/statistics/employment/jobpat-eeo1/2010/index.cfm#select_label

Valverde, L. A. (2003). *Leaders of color in higher education: Unrecognized triumphs in harsh institutions*. Walnut Creek, CA: AltaMira Press.

Vickers, M., & Parris, M. (2007). Your job no longer exists: From experiences of alienation to experience of resilience--a phenomenological study. *Employee Responsibility & Rights Journal*, 19(2), 113-125.

Walker, J. W., & LaRocco, J. M. (2004; January-February). Succession management and the board. *The Corporate Board, 25*(144), 10.

Wang, X. T. (2004). Self-framing of risky choice. *Journal of Behavioral Decision Making, 17*, 7-23.

Wickens, C. D., Lee, J.D., Liu, Y., & Becker, S. E. (2004). *An introduction to human factors engineering.* New York, NY: Prentice Hall.

Wolf, J. H. (2007). The role and impact of person-organization fit in the selection interview with senior level candidates. (Doctoral dissertation, Fielding Graduate University, Santa Barbara, CA). *ProQuest Dissertations & Theses (PQDT).*

Yechiam, E., Druyan, M., & Ert, E. (2008). Observing others' behavior and risk taking in decisions from experience. *Judgment and Decision Making, 3*, 493-500.

Zsambok, C. E., & Klein, G. (Eds.). (1997). *Naturalistic decision making*. Mahwah, NJ: Lawrence Erlbaum Associates.

APPENDICES

APPENDIX A

EMAIL LETTER TO PARTICIPANTS

Date:

Dear NAME:

I am Roy Whitmore and I am completing my Ph.D. at Fielding Graduate University, and I would like you to participate in my dissertation study. In addition to my studies I am a former Vice President of operations for SuperValu Company. I currently own an executive recruiting business and I teach part-time at DePaul University.

I am conducting a research study to better understand how senior executives (CEOs / presidents) define their decision making process for selecting their senior-level direct reports to better understand the elements of their decision-making process including how they use heuristics during their decision-making process. Heuristics are the cognitive short cuts we access during our decision-making process. Previously, the vast majority of research in this area has focused on group decision-making at the executive level and has been completed in. We believe that its time to hear from those that actually make the final decision regarding how they describe their decision making process when selecting their subordinates.

Your knowledge of selecting and developing leaders would be extremely valuable to our research and the vast amount of literature in the decision-making discipline. Additionally, this research could have a profound influence regarding how senior executives are selected in the future and this information will serve as important preparation guidelines for those seeking higher positions in leadership. As you know all participants identity will remain anonymous unless he/she agree to have their identity released.

I am hopeful that you can allow 60 minutes of your valuable time to support this important study. If you are not available will you recommend a peer or subordinate (CFO, COO), or a retired CEO, president, or board member that is willing to support our scholarly offering to the history of leadership and decision making?

Thanks

Roy Whitmore
Faculty

DePaul University | School for New Learning | SNL Online
1 East Jackson Boulevard | Chicago IL 60604
Rwhitmor@depaul.edu | (630) 585-7702) or (630) 251-0352

APPENDIX B

FOLLOW UP LETTER TO PARTICIPANTS

DATE

NAME

DEAR (NAME)

    I wanted to check in with you to determine if you had a chance to review my email requesting your participation in my dissertation study. Though the request is for 60 minutes of your time I believe that we can complete the interview in less time if that is a concern, and I can adjust my schedule to speak at your convenience.
    I assure you that your participation in the study is confidential and there will be no negative impact as confirmed by the IRB at Fielding Graduate University.
    If interested, please let me know and we can coordinate calendars. I do thank you in advance for considering my request.
Regards,

Roy

Roy whitmore
Ph.D. student
Fielding Graduate University
Attachment:
Original email request
Informed consent form.

APPENDIX C

THANK YOU EMAIL LETTER TO PARTICIPANTS WITH COPY OF TRANSCRIPTION

DATE

NAME

DEAR (NAME)

I wanted to offer you the opportunity to review the audio tape transcribed of your interview this fall in my dissertation study on the decision making process of senior executives when selecting senior-level direct reports. Attached you will find the file for your review and edit.

Please take a moment to review and return with any edits or comments. I would appreciate a response in a week because I am completing the findings sections of my dissertation.

I did want to thank you again for your participation in my study. I have completed all of my dissertation interviews and will complete the analysis of the data in the next month. If all goes well I will graduate this spring and I will send you a copy of my final dissertation. Thanks again!!!
Regards,

Roy
Roy Whitmore
Ph.D. student
Fielding Graduate University

Attachment:
Transcription

APPENDIX D

Interview Protocol

Participants were asked the following:

1) Think about the process you have used in making hiring and promotion decisions the last few years. Focus on a hiring event that you experienced as going well, someone that was successful, and tell me a bit about what you were thinking, how you were assessing and evaluating that candidate. What elements of the process caused you to believe that you should hire or promote this individual? It would help if you would simply think about one event and then tell a story about the experience. I may occasionally ask you specific related questions as we go through the process.

2) Tell me a story about a hiring event that did not work out well, one in which the person that you hired or promoted was not successful and you realized later that you had hired or promoted the wrong person. Tell me why you think your decision to hire this individual was flawed. Do you have someone in mind that you can speak about?

Appendix E

Transcriptionist Confidentiality Agreement

Thank you for agreeing to participate in the research study entitled How Senior Executives Define Their Decision Making Process When Selecting Subordinates. Please read and sign the agreement below.

I, _____, agree to transcribe data for this study. I agree that I will:

1. Keep all research information shared with me confidential by not discussing or sharing the information in any form or format (e. g., disks, tapes, transcripts) with anyone other that Roy Whitmore, the primary researcher of the study;
2. Keep all research information in any form or format (e. g., disks, tapes, transcripts) secure while it is in my passion. This includes:
   - Using closed headphones when transcribing audiotaped interviews;
   - Keeping all transcripts documents and digitized interviews in computer password protected files;
   - Closing any transcription programs and documents when temporarily away from the computer;
   - Keeping any printed transcripts in a secure location such as a locked file cabinet; and
   - Permanently deleting any e-mail communication containing the data;
3. Give all research information in any form or format (e.g., disks, tapes, transcripts) to the primary researcher when I have completed the research tasks;
4. Erase or destroy all research information in any form or format that is not returnable to the primary researcher (e.g., information stored on my computer hard drive) upon completion of the research tasks.

Signed,   Date

Appendix F

Fielding Graduate University Informed

Consent Form

Toward Understanding the Decision Making Process of Senior Executives When Selecting Subordinates

NAME OF SUBJECT: How Senior Executives Use Heuristics During Their Decision-Making Process For Selecting Senior-Level Direct Reports

You have been asked to participate in a research study conducted by Roy Whitmore, a doctoral student in the School of Human and Organizational Development at Fielding Graduate University, Santa Barbara, CA. Barbara Mink EdD supervises this study. This research involves the study of Fortune 1000 CEOs and Presidents' decision making process when selecting subordinates and is part of Roy Whitmore's Fielding doctoral dissertation. You are being asked to participate in this study because you are or were a CEO or President of a Fortune 1000 organization.

Before you agree to participate in this research study, it is important that you read and understand the information provided in this informed consent form. If you have any questions, please ask the researcher for clarification.

Why Is This Study Being Done?

The purpose of this research is to better understand cognitively the **decision making process of senior executives and how they use heuristics during their decision-making process to select senior-level executives as their direct reports.** A vast amount of research dealing with human judgment and decision making has been at the group level. However, there remains a void in the literature in how senior executives make subordinate selection decisions after interviewing qualified candidates. As such, your input could be valuable in assisting researcher and scholars in their effort to better understand this phenomenon.

Your part will consist of one interview that will last approximately 60 minutes.

How Many People Will Take Part In The Study?

No more than 15 senior executives from Fortune 1000 organizations will take part in this study.

What Is Involved In The Study?

If you agree to participate in this study, you will participate in one phone interview that will last one and one half hour consisting two core questions.

How Long Will I Be In The Study?

The study involves one-telephone interviews to be arranged at your convenience. This will last approximately 60 minutes for the first interview and no more than 30 minutes for the second interview. The total time involved in participation will be approximately one hour.

What Are The Risks Of The Study?

This research has no measurable risk for you as a participant as confirmed by the IRB.

What Are The Benefits Of The Study?

You may develop greater personal awareness of new interviewing techniques that can improve your decision making process when selecting direct reports in the future, and you may better understand the reasons that might have guided your decision to select direct reports as a result of your participation in this research.

What About Confidentiality and Protection?

Study related records are held in confidence. Your consent to participate in this study includes consent for the researcher, supervising faculty, and possibly a confidential Research Assistant to review your data. Your research records may also be inspected by authorized representatives of Fielding Graduate University, including members of the Institutional Review Board or their designees. They may inspect, and photocopy, as needed, your records for study monitoring or auditing purposes. In addition, parts of your record may be photocopied.

The information you provide will be kept strictly confidential. The informed consent forms and other identifying information will be kept separate from the data. All material will be kept in a safe located in the researcher's home. Only the researcher, Barbara Mink EdD my committee supervisor, possible a confidential Research Assistant, who has signed the attached Professional Assistance Confidentiality Agreement, will listen to the tape recordings. I will destroy any records that would identify you as a participant in this study, such as informed consent forms, approximately three years after the study is complete.

You will be assigned a number that will be used for direct quotes included in the final research report. If any direct quotes will be used, permission will be sought from you first.

The results of this research will be published in my dissertation and possibly published in subsequent journals, books, or presentations. Your name and identifying information will not be used in any publications.

The security of data transmitted over the Internet cannot be guaranteed; therefore, there is a slight risk that the information you send to me via email will not be secure. The collection of such data is not expected to present any greater risk than you would encounter in everyday life when sending and/or receiving information over the Internet.

Participation In Research Is Voluntary:

You are free to decline to participate or to withdraw from this study at any time, either during or after your participation, without negative consequences. Should you withdraw, your data will be eliminated from the study and will be destroyed.

The researcher is also free to terminate the study at any time.

Compensation:

No compensation will be provided for participation.

Additional Information:

If you have any questions about any aspect of this study or your involvement, please tell the Researcher before signing this form. You may also contact the supervising faculty if you have questions or concerns your participation in this study. The supervising faculty has provided contact information at the bottom of this form.

You may also ask questions at any time during your participation in this study.

If at any time you have questions or concerns about your rights as a research participant, contact the Fielding Graduate University IRB by email at irb@fielding.edu or by telephone at 805-898-

4033.

Two copies of this informed consent form have been provided. Please sign both, indicating you have read, understood, and agree to participate in this research. Return one to the researcher and keep the other for your files. The Institutional Review Board of Fielding Graduate University retains the right to access to all signed informed consent forms.

I have read the above informed consent document and have had the opportunity to ask questions about this study. I have been told my rights as a research participant, and I voluntarily consent to participate in this study. By signing this form, I agree to participate in this research study. I shall receive a signed and dated copy of this consent.

_____
NAME OF PARTICIPANT (please print)

_____
SIGNATURE OF PARTICIPANT

_____
DATE

Barbara Mink EdD,	Roy Whitmore,
Fielding Graduate University	Fielding Graduate University
2112 Santa Barbara Street	2462 Waterside Drive
Santa Barbara, CA 93105	Aurora, IL 60502
805-687-1099	630-585-7702

Yes, please send a summary of the study results to:

_____
NAME (please print)
_____
Street Address

_____
City, State, Zip

Appendix G

Categories and Heuristics Relationship

Categories From Codes	Availability heuristics	Representative Heuristics	Confirmation Bias	Overconfidence Bias
Personality Fit		X	X	X
Collaboration	X	X	X	X
Leadership Style		X	X	X
Cultural Fit	X	X	X	X
Previous Contributions	X	X	X	X
Experience	X	X	X	
Communication Skills	X	X	X	
High Desire to Work in the Organization	X	X	X	
Ego	X	X	X	
Smart / Strategic		X	X	
Values Fit	X	X	X	
Education		X	X	
Team Player	X	X	X	
Testing			X	
Positive Attitude	X	X	X	
Job Fit	X	X	X	

APPENDIX H

CODING OF STUDY RESULTS

Themes: Cultural Fit, Personality Fit, Job Fit, Experience, Previous Contributions, Collaboration, Education, Communication, Desire, Ego, Smart-Strategic, Team Player, Leadership Style, Values, Testing,

Core Category 1: Rational and Naturalistic Decision-Making

Core Category 2: Organization Culture and Heuristics

Core Category 3: Personality and Leadership Style

Core Category 4: Experience, Previous Contributions, and Education

Core Category 5: Senior Executives Overconfidence Bias

APPENDIX H

ATLAS.ti RELATED DATA AND FAMILY OF CODES

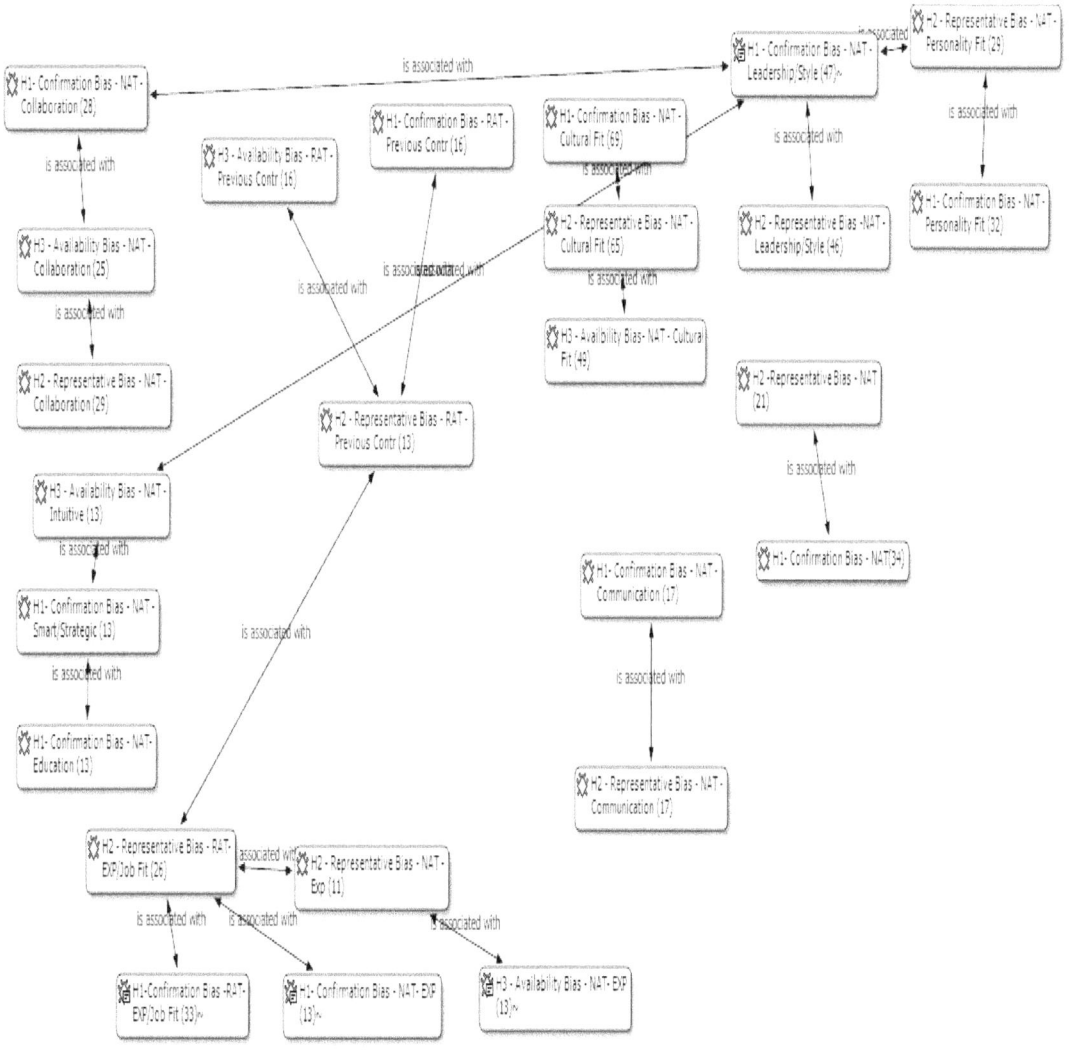

www.ingramcontent.com/pod-product-compliance
Lightning Source LLC
Chambersburg PA
CBHW080252180526
45167CB00006B/2506